TRUE TALES
of
AURORA
ILLINOIS

Mysterious Murders, Presidential Visits and
Blues Legends in the City of Lights

Matt Hanley

THE
History
PRESS

Published by The History Press
Charleston, SC 29403
www.historypress.net

Back cover image courtesy of the Aurora Historical Society.

First published 2012

ISBN 978.1.60949.539.8

Library of Congress CIP data applied for

Notice: The information in this book is true and complete to the best of our knowledge. It is offered without guarantee on the part of the author or The History Press. The author and The History Press disclaim all liability in connection with the use of this book.

Contents

Acknowledgements

This book would not have been possible without the assistance and patience of many people. At the *Beacon-News*, editors Mike Cetera, Denise Crosby, Tom Johnson, Rick Nagel, Andre Salles and Nikki Roller found errors, asked questions, encouraged my reporting and made insightful edits. A writer is a fool without great editors. I am lucky to work with such talented people. Beacon librarian Trish Hard tracked thousands of files that were invaluable to my reporting. Photographer Brian Powers performed computer wizardry that made the photos visible. Gratitude should also be extended to Sun-Times Media publisher John Barron for making versions of stories previously published in the *Beacon-News* available. Finally, a thank-you is not enough for John Russell, the best city editor in America, who inspires me to be a better reporter every day.

Aurora Historical Society Executive Director John Jaros (aurorahistory. net) is mentioned in the bibliography several times, but special mention needs to be made of his contributions. Jaros knows the details and context of Aurora's history better than anyone and was a regular, generous resource for me. Every time I had a question, he had an answer. Thank you.

The publishers at The History Press were supportive and open to my ideas. I looked around: they are publishing the best local history books anywhere. Check them out at historypress.net.

A special thanks to the people who told me their stories, especially the Perez family, Ann Prestero, Marcia Mount, Audre' Grometer and Billy Boy Arnold. Some stories were painful; all were personal. I am grateful you allowed me to share them.

ACKNOWLEDGEMENTS

Finally, a thank-you to my family. My mom (who was my first proofreader) and my dad (who inspired my love of history) allowed me to go into journalism when banking would have guaranteed a better retirement home. Most importantly: my beautiful wife, Lynne, and my son, Mark, allowed me to stay up late plinking away at a computer. Thank you, Lynne, for copyediting 37,063 words and convincing me someone else would want to read them. Thank you, Mark, for being a source of stress relief and for suggesting that I "use vowels" in my book, which turned out to be an excellent suggestion. I hope someday you write a book twice as good.

Founding Brothers

Joseph McCarty was twenty-four when he left his home in Elmira, New York heading for history.

Soldiers returning from the Black Hawk War had told Joseph and his brother, Samuel, about the beauty of Illinois. The stories must have sparked some great urge in the brothers. They gambled on the unknown for a chance to claim their own land in the Wild West.

"In every little community that started, there was someone like the McCartys," said John Jaros, executive director of the Aurora Historical Society. "It was one of those eras you could be a self-made man. If you wanted to change your fortune, you could migrate. To better your fortunes, you went west. In the 1830s, Illinois was the West."

And so, on November 25, 1833, Joseph set out on a journey that would change his life and shape the Fox Valley.

He crossed the Allegheny River and then stopped to build a canoe that he rode through rapids and carried around dams. He abandoned the canoe and booked passage on a steamer bound for the Mississippi. He spent the winter in Missouri, working odd jobs. And he didn't forget about Illinois, the land to which he had mapped a course.

Finally, after the thaw, Joseph made it to Ottawa. There, he hired a prospector to help look for a spot for his mill. In April 1834, the two traveled forty miles toward the Fox River. Thin, well-worn Indian trails crossed tiny paths through the vast prairie. A great wooded area stretched along the river, ending near where the river split for an island—the ideal place for a dam.

Samuel McCarty. There are no known pictures of Joseph McCarty. *From the collection of the Aurora Historical Society.*

Joseph laid claim to 860 acres on both sides of the river. Then he wrote home.

The letter has not survived, but whatever Joseph said to his little brother convinced Samuel that the good life was available in Illinois. By November 1834, Samuel had joined his brother along the Fox River.

Their life was focused on economic opportunity. They looked at the things they needed and figured others would need them, too.

The brothers cut logs for homes at their lumber mill. By 1835, they were plotting out streets and land parcels, including a park on the east side of the river that would later be named in their honor.

In 1836, the brothers persuaded stagecoach drivers to divert the route to Chicago from Montgomery to Aurora.

"This was beyond doubt a turning point in the history of Aurora," the *Beacon-News* wrote in Samuel's obituary.

Although he arrived first, Joseph's history in Aurora would not be a long or happy one. In August 1838, he was threatened with tuberculosis and headed south. Less than a year later, he died on his way to Alabama at the age of thirty-one.

But Samuel carried on. He was never elected to any public office, but he became the unofficial leader of Aurora. He was consulted on important decisions and donated lands that would be used for schools and churches. He lived until 1899, long enough to see the town that started with his mill become a thriving city.

McCarty Mills as seen in 1858, more than two decades after Samuel and Joseph McCarty settled in Aurora. *From the collection of the Aurora Historical Society.*

"It's almost like these first few were kind of ahead of the curve," Jaros said. "They knew it was coming. It was just going to be a matter of time before people were going to flock there."

So how did Aurora get its name?

In 1834, when someone wanted to mail a letter to someone living in the area that would later be called Aurora, they had plenty of options for addresses.

Addressing it "Aunt Mabel at Fox River, Illinois," probably would have made it. So would "Aunt Mabel at Fox Woods, Illinois." By 1835, after Samuel and Joseph McCarty put up the city's first mill, the letter could be mailed to "McCarty's Mill" or "McCarty Mills."

In 1837, when the first post office was established, residents chose the name "Waubonsie," (sometimes spelled Waubansie) after the Indian chief that many of the residents knew and respected.

So, how did the town end up as Aurora? There are two theories on that.

The first theory involves New York. One prominent citizen, E.D. Terry, was from an area of New York called Aurora. In the 1830s, the government ran ads in East Coast newspapers, such as "Sell your farm and buy four times as much land in the Midwest! One dollar an acre!"

Chief Waubonsie. Beacon-News *archives.*

The Black Hawk War had cleared the way for white settlers to move west. Men returned home with tales of fertile ground near the Fox River, and New Yorkers headed to Illinois. They brought their town names with them. In New York alone, you can visit Aurora, Oswego, Batavia, Geneva, Hinckley, Montgomery, Newark, Virgil, Yorkville and Millbrook. It may seem strange that these pioneers would borrow names already in use. Montgomery historian Debbie Buchanan provided a reasonable explanation for doing so.

"Back in those days, when you said goodbye to your family, you were pretty much saying goodbye for good. Elderly parents at home—you may never see them again," she said. "So I think there was probably a lot of nostalgia."

The second theory on how Aurora received its name is the more intellectual version: In Pottawatomie tongue, Waubonsie means "morning light or break of day." So, local residents borrowed the Roman goddess of dawn's moniker.

When asked whether that second theory might be revisionist history, Jaros stays neutral. "I don't take sides. I really don't know," he said.

For a while, the west side of the river was called West Aurora and the east side just plain Aurora. By 1857, both sides had joined, and the name Aurora has remained essentially unchallenged since.

Abraham Lincoln and the Aurora Water Wheel Case

In 1854, attorney Abraham Lincoln found himself again infected with the political bug.

After a few years away from politics, a misstep by U.S. senator Stephen Douglas of Illinois had pulled Lincoln back to the political arena. Lincoln was ready to run for the Senate but felt the need to be assured he had the support of other Illinois legislators.

Lincoln started sending letters to old friends, former clients and political allies. When he came to Kane County, Lincoln reached out to a man who was all three: Aurora merchant Charles Hoyt.

Years earlier, Hoyt and Lincoln had come together on a curious case that taxed Lincoln's legal talents. Now, on the cusp of launching his historic political career, Lincoln made sure to contact his old Aurora friend. "You used to express a great deal of partiality for me," Lincoln wrote in his November 10, 1854 letter to Hoyt. "And if you are still so, now is the time. Some friends here are really for me for the U.S. Senate; and I should be very grateful if you could make a mark for me among your members."

Lincoln's first work as an elected official had been exciting, albeit ultimately discouraging. As a member of the U.S. House of Representatives, the freshman congressman isolated himself by arguing against the Mexican-American War.

Rebuffed, Lincoln found comfort in returning to the court system. He rode the judicial circuit in central Illinois, arguing large and small legal cases and becoming well known and financially stable. He also earned a reputation for his fierce honesty and well-crafted closing arguments.

He might have stayed in law if, in 1854, Douglas had not supported legislation allowing new northern territories to decide whether they wanted to be free or slave states. Before Douglas's bill, Lincoln had already spoken out against slavery as both an "injustice and bad policy," but he assumed the problem would solve itself. Lincoln believed Douglas's bill would spread, not contain, slavery.

So, in 1854, Lincoln started seeking the Whig Party's nomination. Since senators were elected by state legislators, Lincoln used a letter-writing campaign—including the letter he wrote to Hoyt—to gauge his Illinois support. Lincoln trusted Hoyt; the two men had met more than five years earlier, when, strangely enough, Hoyt was sued for stealing the patent on an Ohio man's water wheel.

"WILLING TO PAY A GOOD FEE"

Charles Hoyt was born in Massachusetts in 1797 and learned the milling trade from his father while the family still lived in the East.

After selling his interests in an Ohio furnace company in 1841, Hoyt came to Aurora, most likely attracted by the Fox River, a powerful magnet for enterprising businessmen.

On the east bank was McCarty Mills, started by Aurora's founding brothers, Joseph and Samuel McCarty. Hoyt built Black Hawk Mills almost directly across the river.

Black Hawk was called the largest and best mill in the state. Its huge water wheels used the river's powerful current to turn the mills that ground corn and grain into flour—the very process that would eventually bring Lincoln and Hoyt together.

Hoyt's success attracted jealousy and competition and, in 1849, he was sued by Zebulon Parker, a miller from Ohio. Twenty years earlier, Parker had invented a water wheel with both curved spouts and square boxes to catch the water. Parker believed those boxes made his mill unique—and therefore protected by copyright. Parker had even succeeded in extracting royalties from mill owners across the country.

When Parker heard Hoyt was using a similar wheel without paying royalties, Parker sued for patent infringement. Hoyt hired Grant Goodrich, a Chicago attorney who would later help start Northwestern University. Mill operators across the Midwest followed the case, wondering if they too would face suits for their water wheels.

But shortly before the case was to be argued in Springfield, Goodrich's wife became severely ill. Goodrich recommended a friend take his place on the water wheel suit, a tall forty-year-old Springfield lawyer who had recently left Congress.

"I have advised Mr. Chas Hoit [sic] to employ you in the case of Patent violation," Goodrich wrote to Lincoln on May 24, 1849. "It is an important case & Hoit is willing to pay a good fee."

In some respects, Lincoln was an odd choice for a complicated patent case; the entirety of his formal schooling added up to just 18 months. But Lincoln had an insatiable curiosity. Goodrich also knew Lincoln was a powerful speaker, a man who could reduce difficult concepts to understandable terms. But despite Goodrich's faith in him, Lincoln lost the case in Springfield. He immediately motioned for a new case to be heard in Chicago.

Hoyt apparently had little doubt about who would represent him when the water wheel case came up for appeal. Lincoln would get another chance.

"Gratifying Triumph"

The water wheel case was problematic because it involved not only the technical aspects of patent law—and uncertainty over who "owned" intellectual property—but also the mechanics and physics of hydropower. Lincoln had to convince the jury that Parker's wheel was no different than hundreds of other mill wheels: Parker's modifications were insignificant, not brilliant.

While Lincoln stayed on Hoyt's case, the July 1850 trial generated little interest in Hoyt's hometown.

The *Beacon-News*, consumed with news about the death of President Zachary Taylor, made little note of the two-week trial. The brief item about the outcome of the water wheel received barely more space in the paper than another notice, printed a few days later, highlighting Mr. Edwin Booth's acting talent in a "very credible" performance in a recent play. (No mention was made of Edwin's youngest brother, John Wilkes, who was also an actor.)

But Lincoln's performance in the courtroom was dazzling.

"The trial lasted several days and Lincoln manifested great interest," Goodrich would later recall. "[Lincoln] had run, or aided in running a saw mill, and explained in this argument the action of water on the wheel in a manner so clear and intelligible that the jury were enabled to comprehend the points and line of defense without the least difficulty."

But when the jury went out, Lincoln—who, at the same time, was writing a eulogy for President Taylor—started to worry. After two hours, he ran into one of the jurors. The man held up one finger, which Lincoln took as a sign that the other eleven were against him.

As he fretted, Lincoln talked about a Tazewell County, Illinois jury that almost went against him. It had been a divorce case, and Lincoln represented a woman who was seeking to get away from her "gross, morose, fault-finding and uncomfortable" husband.

Lincoln couldn't prove the woman had been physically abused, a legal standard for divorce. But in deliberations, one juror spoke up.

"'Gentleman, I am going to lie down to sleep,'" Lincoln quoted the man saying. "'And when you get ready to give a verdict for that little woman, then wake me up...for not before will I give a verdict against her will I lie here till I rot.'"

Lincoln concluded that if the Hoyt juror could have the strength of that Tazewell juryman, they were safe.

"Strange to relate the jury did come in with a verdict for [Hoyt]," Goodrich wrote. "Lincoln always regarded it as one of the gratifying triumphs of his professional life."

"He Was So Tall"

Did Lincoln need to see the mills in person to prove his case? No obvious record exists of a visit to Aurora, save one eyewitness account of an encounter in Hoyt's store.

With the mill so successful and Aurora growing (the town already had almost 1,900 residents), Hoyt opened a general store that promised "by far the largest and best assortment of Groceries and fancy jewelry."

"To attempt an enumeration of the various articles would be superfluous," one ad bragged of the store's stock. "The subscribers can only say that his stock will be found most perfect. Persons wishing to buy will do well to call and examine before purchasing elsewhere."

And so, it was in that store during the summer of 1851 (according to legend anyway) that Isabelle Landry met the future president.

As Landry, age ten, was leaving, she ran into a local judge and a tall, lanky stranger.

"Naturally, I took little detailed notice of him, but he attracted my attention for the fact that he was so tall and wore such a high hat," she told

River Street in 1867. Charles Hoyt's store is on the right. Although Abraham Lincoln likely visited an earlier version of Hoyt's store, the muddy streets and wooden sidewalks would have looked familiar. *From the collection of the Aurora Historical Society.*

the *Beacon-News* in 1928. "[The] sleeves on his coat...were somewhat too short for him."

Hoyt happened to mention that the little girl could sing in French, and Landry happily performed an impromptu concert for the men. Afterward, Lincoln took the girl's hand, complimented her and bought her a pound of candy. The judge, not to be outdone, also bought a pound of candy for the girl.

The historical record doesn't support the timeline Landry gives—Lincoln was in southern Illinois in the summer of 1851—but it doesn't eliminate the possibility. It's reasonable to believe that, having worked with Hoyt, Lincoln would have stopped in Aurora at some point.

It's as close as Aurora may ever come to providing a witness of Lincoln stepping on city soil.

"Let This Be Confidential"

By 1854, Hoyt was a retired elder statesman in Aurora, respected for his business and political advice. It's no surprise that among the many letters Lincoln sent while seeking a Senate seat, he called on Hoyt.

"Please write me at all events, giving me the names, post office and political position of members round about you," Lincoln wrote in that November 10, 1854 letter. "Let this be confidential."

Hoyt went to work immediately. Ten days later, he wrote back to Lincoln with some recommendations of local Whig loyalists.

"Will do all I can for you for let me asure [sic] you," Hoyt wrote. "It would give me great pleasure to see you in the U.S. Senate."

Hoyt didn't forget about his own concerns, either. Parker had appealed the second verdict.

"What is to be done with my Water Wheel Sute?" Hoyt asked. "Have we got to triy that matter again if so pleas examin the matter and see that our paps air all as they should be."

Lincoln would not be the party nominee in 1854. After a close vote, he stepped aside to ensure that an anti-slavery candidate, Lyman Trumbull, would be nominated. Trumbull won the general election; Lincoln gained political capital.

Probably much to Hoyt's relief, Lincoln put an end to the water wheel headache in an 1855 letter, now in the possession of the Aurora Historical Society. Lincoln told Hoyt he had succeeded in getting the second appeal dismissed.

"Parker is broken up and seems to be doing nothing about his cases," Lincoln assured Hoyt. "From all this, I suppose the cases are not very likely to be reinstated."

Abraham Lincoln's signature on a letter to Charles Hoyt. *From the collection of the Aurora Historical Society.*

Postscript

In 1858, Lincoln again ran for Senate, a campaign that, though unsuccessful, would launch him into the national spotlight through a series of stirring debates with Stephen A. Douglas.

In June 1858, Lincoln delivered one of the most important addresses of his career at the Illinois Republican Convention.

"A house divided against itself cannot stand," Lincoln said. He then drew a thick political line between Douglas's views and his own. "I believe this government cannot endure permanently half slave and half free. It will become all one thing or all the other."

The words remain a landmark for Lincoln. But later, in a lesser-known section of the speech, Lincoln drew an interesting metaphor. He was trying to show that his rivals had secretly worked behind the scenes against the slavery issue. Although he could offer no concrete proof, Lincoln asked the audience to decide for themselves if there was evidence of premeditation.

"When we see a lot of framed timbers, different portions of which we know have been gotten out at different times and places and by different workmen... and when we see these timbers joined together and see they exactly make the frame of a house or a mill...all the lengths and proportions of the different pieces exactly adapted to their respective places...in such a case, we find it impossible not to believe that...all worked upon a common plan."

It would be nice (though wholly speculative) to imagine that as Abraham Lincoln concluded one of the most important speeches in U.S. history—a speech that compared political maneuvering to the precision of a water mill—he couldn't help remember one of his old legal cases: the curious suit against Charles Hoyt's well-made Aurora water wheel.

A City of Lights

H is true feelings on the issue are not recorded, but John Loser must have been aggravated at the state of River Street in 1908. Businesses were failing. Stores that had once been city landmarks were disappearing.

Loser, a veteran grocer, must have reminisced about the street he once knew, which was once the bustling economic center of a new city on the Fox River.

Now, Broadway—all the way on the other side of the river!—was Aurora's heart.

Each night, large crowds would leave the West Side and head across the bridges to see shows in one of the five theaters and opera houses on the East Side.

Appalling.

The West Side had tried to respond, holding band concerts on Saturday nights. But it was going to take more than a few tunes to change the tide.

Loser (pronounced Low-sir) must have known a bold move was needed, something to catch the imagination of the shopping public. Something to show those east-siders there was plenty of life in both halves of town.

Cartoonists like to portray the moment of inspiration as a light bulb suddenly illuminating above the inspired individual's head. Perhaps at the meeting of the West Side Improvement Association in August 1908, the metaphorical became literal.

The idea they chose that evening would change the city in unexpected ways. And it may have even, for at least a little while, bridged Aurora's greatest gap, the one between two sides of a river.

AN ECONOMIC SHIFT

It was, of course, the Fox River that brought people to Aurora in the first place. Joseph and Samuel McCarty saw this meandering waterway as the perfect place to set up a sawmill. Three years after they arrived, McCarty's Mill became Aurora. Well, the East Side, at least. The West Side? That was another place, another land. Over there, the town would be called West Aurora, an appendage of the real deal. It would take fifteen years for both sides to join under one name.

The river has never united as much as it has divided. Somehow, the town never really outgrew the simple pettiness that came with looking across the banks and sticking out your tongue. The east and west sides of Aurora seemed destined to live as brothers: they loved each other and defended against outsiders but never, ever stopped trying to outshine each other.

So it was natural the two streets that paralleled the Fox, River Street on the west and Broadway on the east, became economic rivals.

In the 1870s and '80s, River Street was dominant. Rather than drive cattle and hogs to Chicago markets, farmers from as far away as Leland would make the three-day trip to Aurora, where the animals could be bought, slaughtered and shipped. Wagons stretched a half mile with farmers lined up to sell livestock.

That climate attracted hearty young businessmen like Loser. Born in Germany, he came to the U.S. in 1864 at the age of eighteen. He worked for a few years as a farmer and a stonecutter until he started working at his uncle's grocery store on the West Side. Loser, a thin, mustachioed man, eschewed politics, but he took pride in his community projects, joining civic boards and assisting the city's water department. But time and technology did not

John Loser. *From the collection of the Aurora Historical Society.*

favor Loser or the west bank. Improved railroads soon made it easy to skip Aurora and get live animals into the city.

By 1908, Aurora was stepping out of its small-town shoes: a U.S. senator called Aurora home; street signs had been added to the intersections to assist out-of-town visitors; the city's banks recorded more than $4.8 million in deposits—half a million more than either Elgin or Joliet.

And the east side of the river had been in prime position to take advantage of the changes. As the economy shifted away from agriculture, dry goods stores and banks popped up along Broadway.

More importantly, when the lines were laid for interurban cars—small electric trains that connected towns in the Fox Valley—they stopped on the East Side. Many visitors probably wandered into Alschuler Brothers, the magnificent three-story building at 17 South Broadway that was one of the finest clothing stores in the Midwest.

The three Alschuler brothers opened their clothing store in 1885. At that time, the street was unpaved and muddy. The sidewalks were made of wood. Like Loser on the other side, Alschuler became a civic leader, if not a political one. To draw people in, he lit his store with electric lights, which was unheard of at the time.

FREE INSTALLATION

Until then, Aurora's streets were illuminated by dim, flickering gaslights. But Loser had brainstormed a dramatic plan. To spark the public's imagination, the West Side Improvement Association would line the city streets with electric lights.

The plan was ingenious because it was not only practical, but if it worked, it might be profitable, too. The idea was not unique, except in its application. In Chicago, Milwaukee Avenue store owners strung thousands of lights outside their stores, prompting others to call it "The Great White Way."

But for towns the size of Aurora, an all-electric municipal light system would be spectacular. The city had gained acclaim in 1881 for becoming the first town to light a city with electric lights, putting light towers on top of six buildings. It was novel, if not necessarily effective.

"This is a very fine light where it shines, but awful poor in the shade," reported the *Beacon-News*. "At one place you may tell the time by your watch and ten feet further, fall into the ditch."

A City of Lights

With electric lights lining the streets on the West Side, night would turn into day. The $60 light poles turned out by the American Wood Working Company were 14 feet tall and carried three new tungsten light bulbs, which promised to emit an amazing 208 candles' worth of light.

After announcing their plan, Loser and other West Side merchants forfeited their free time in the spirit of civic pride. Loser, sixty-two years old, was constantly on the streets with his younger counterparts laying pipe, working with cement mixers and soliciting funds. Invitations were sent out across the Fox Valley.

The sacrifices were worth it.

Promptly at 7:00 p.m. on November 21, 1908—with residents from Aurora, Batavia, Geneva, St. Charles, Oswego and Yorkville celebrating—$8,000 worth of lights paid for by residents' donations were turned on and then handed over to the city. Mayor E.C. Finch accepted the lights, but he was no dummy: he surely knew any celebration on the West Side, no matter how spectacular, could be seen as an affront to his constituency on the east side of town. He chose his words carefully.

"I believe an era of prosperity is at our door such as we have never seen before," Finch told the crowd. "I want it understood that this is one city and one people. We are all looking forward to added growth and development of Aurora and the great majority of people are working together for the common development of the city's interests. We should have no East Side and no West Side but should all root for Aurora."

The party went on well past midnight. Observers predicted the West Side would be the lively side of town now.

Five days later, the city's namesake high schools would play on Hurd Island, which was neutral territory. West fans yelled "U Rah! U Rah!" while east-siders responded with "Osky Wow Wow! Skinny wow wow EAHS Wow!" The game ended in a 6–6 tie.

It was the only sort of dead heat east-siders would allow. The West Side's one-upmanship simply would not stand. Within a few hours of the West Side's celebration, the East Aurora Improvement Association announced plans to light their side of the city. They would also donate the lights to the city, only theirs would be better, with brighter lights, and there would be more of them. And fireworks. And a parade.

"A DANDY TOWN"

In just three weeks, East Side merchants tore out dozens of streetcar and gas-line poles to make way for their light poles, already being turned out by the American Wood Working Company, a lucky benefactor of this municipal competition. Electricians got sick of working in the dark, in the rain and in the snow. If the West Side's show was wonderful, the East Side's would have to be spectacular. The West Side's lights had cost $8,000; the East's cost $12,000. The West Side's poles had three globes; the East's boasted five.

At the heart of the East Side's efforts was Harry Alschuler, the veteran owner of Northern Illinois's finest clothing store. At fifty-one, Alschuler, a thin, distinguished looking man, was out day and night soliciting contributions from business owners. On December 17, the lights were ready. The night

"Nominate the Man Who Can Win in November"

SAMUEL ALSCHULER

Democratic Candidate For

GOVERNOR

Primaries: Tuesday, April 9, 1912

Relatives of the Alschuler family remain prominent to this day. Pictured is a poster from Sam Alschuler's unsuccessful gubernatorial campaign. *From the collection of the Aurora Historical Society.*

was muggy and damp, and city officials worried no one would venture out for the ceremony. But fifteen thousand people showed up. At 7:30 p.m., as fireworks boomed and whistles blasted, sixteen blocks of Broadway were lit. Spectators in the crowd held up banners reading "Aurora beautiful city of light" and "First in 1882, still there in 1908." A young boy was so impressed he blurted out, within earshot of Mayor Finch, "Gee, ain't Aurora a dandy town."

And for that day, it surely was.

Some West Side merchants even closed their stores to attend the gala, for they knew the difference between a feud and a friendly competition.

"There is not another town in the country nor in the world that I know of whose streets are lighted as those of Aurora now," William Carroll, the electrician for the city of Chicago, told the crowd. "One would not believe a town of this size could so far outstrip not only its equals in population but the larger cities as well."

The lights were an immediate success on both sides of town. Even struggling stores on the West Side reported their biggest sales in five years.

River Street after the installation of the new street lights. *From the collection of the Aurora Historical Society.*

Of course, not all went smoothly. Within a few hours of the lights being turned on, a saloon owner wrote an advertisement for beer on one of the globes. Within a day, an express driver backed his wagon into a pole, breaking two globes. Aldermen quickly drew up ordinances banning ads on globes and forbidding horses to be tied to poles. But the brilliance of a well-lit city had made its mark. James Ferris of the *Joliet Herald* reported back to residents about what he saw.

"The first glimpse Joliet visitors had was a sight into the depths of a Niagara of electricity," Ferris wrote. "Aurora has ever been foremost in light. The way they turned this particular trick was beautiful." Joliet immediately started plans to light its downtown.

In Aurora, John Loser would keep his grocery store open for another five years; Harry Alschuler would work in his store until 1930.

But what Loser and Alschuler built was a feat more spectacular than civic-minded donations. After the two celebrations, the new slogan of a united city was plastered on postcards and signs. For at least a little while, Aurora had become not a town of west-siders and east-siders but simply "The City of Lights."

The Wright Stuff

AURORA, July 5, 1910—When Al Welsh arrived in town, the young aviator spotted William Henderson's oat field almost right away. Like any good ex-Navy man, Welsh had immediately begun preparing for his big air show by scouting spots where he could bail out of his aircraft in case something went wrong.

And by that afternoon, something had gone wrong.

Twenty minutes into his flight, after soaring to the breathtaking height of 850 feet, Welsh's Wright airplane had begun a graceful, swooping dive back toward Aurora's Driving Park. This flight—the most anticipated event in Aurora's history—had already been delayed for days by bad weather. Now 8,000 people were crowded into the stands, ready to be dazzled.

But when Welsh yanked the rudder control lever that was supposed to pull his plane out of the dive, nothing happened.

Welsh tugged again. Nothing. He couldn't turn the plane.

The open-front biplane dropped like a dead bird to 800 feet.

Then to 700 feet.

Perhaps at first, the crowd thought this was part of the show. After all, the twenty-eight-year-old pilot had a reputation as a daredevil, a man who was not afraid of tough flights.

Years earlier, Welsh had arrived at the Wright's shop in Dayton, Ohio, intent on buying his own airplane. When the Wrights refused to sell him one, he joined their new aviation school instead, training alongside Orville Wright and becoming one of the nation's most famous stunt pilots.

600 feet...

Pilot Al Welsh (left). This photo was probably taken while he was training at the Wright Flying School in 1911. *Library of Congress.*

Now a stuck gear was threatening to end Welsh's career very early. While the problem was certainly most poignant and distressing for Welsh, he was not the only person whose fate was tied to the plane that tottered and swerved as it fell toward Aurora.

500 feet...

There were eighty-three businessmen who probably pictured a less absolute but still painful effect of a crash. They had promised to make up any part of the Wright Brothers' appearance fee that was not covered by admission to the three-day spectacle. And if Welsh didn't pull up soon, their investment would crash along with the pilot.

A Wright Brothers' plane flying over Aurora was supposed be the centerpiece of a gala Fourth of July homecoming celebration. Hundreds of ex-Aurorans from across the country were using the holiday weekend to return to their old hometown. By late May, the city had planned a fantastic event. Already on the schedule were drill demonstrations by the famous Aurora Zouaves, three bands, fireworks, a parade and a diver who would leap from a 250-foot-high platform into the Fox River. Aurora also planned to open the impressive new concrete bridges at Fox Street and Downer Place that would span the river.

Still, city leaders were determined to up the ante with an exhibition that was guaranteed to draw not just former Aurorans but visitors from across the region. So on June 3, a committee of three Aurorans arrived in Dayton, Ohio, to make a sales pitch: Would the Wright Company come to Aurora and put on a show of their airships?

At the time, Orville and Wilbur Wright were among the most brilliant and famous men in the world. But even eight years after their famous first flight, Wright planes had never flown in Illinois. Aurora leaders expected

Orville Wright. *Library of Congress.*

that if they could secure a performance, fifty thousand people might flow into the city.

The Wright Brothers' price for an exhibition was a steep $5,000. As a solution, city leaders struck a deal with eighty-three leading businessmen to guarantee the fee. Admissions would repay the investment. At fifty cents for each person, it seemed impossible the businessmen wouldn't recover their money.

Wright plane flights were scheduled for July 2, 4 and 5; the aviators would rest on Sunday, July 3. Aurora made it known that they had bested Chicago in securing the country's flight sensation. Reportedly, fifty thousand pamphlets were sent out to advertise the event.

Of course, from that point forward, almost everything went wrong. And that was before Welsh started his dive.

400 feet...

It wasn't just Aurora businessmen who wanted to save face. The Wright Brothers were at risk if Welsh couldn't save the airship and himself.

By 1910, the brothers were involved in a spectacular legal battle to protect the patents of their invention, which many people felt should be given to the public as a gift. What a change from December 1903, when reports of the Wrights' 120-foot-high, 12-second flight over Kitty Hawk raised few eyebrows. Initially, not many people realized the importance of stabilized, controlled flight. In 1903, the *Beacon-News* ran a six-sentence-long story accompanied by a small illustration about the "airship that flew in North Carolina."

As the Wrights continued to perfect their machines, the public continued to ignore them or doubted the reliability of reports, until 1908, when Wilbur Wright traveled to France. The aviation community there had openly called the brothers liars. But Wilbur shocked Europe with a demonstration of complicated turns and figure-eight patterns. When they returned to the United States, the Wrights were welcomed to the White House. By 1910, everyone believed in the magic of airplanes, but few had seen them fly.

The Wrights were, of course, tinkerers and inventors, not necessarily businessmen. In fact, it wasn't until eight months before their arrival in Aurora that the Wright Company was incorporated. It had two main purposes: to defend patents against copyright violations and to run air shows that would promote sales of airplanes. Rival shows had already emerged, elbowing into the Wrights' airspace.

The brothers split their focus: Wilbur handled the patent lawsuits and business work while Orville traveled with the shows, including riding the train to Aurora with the airplane that Welsh would pilot.

Thus, Welsh's fall could be the Wrights' fall as well. A crash so soon after incorporation would leave a significant stain on the Wrights' airplanes.

300 feet...

The build-up to the Wright flights had not been subtle. The *Beacon-News* provided daily updates of the Wright planes' accomplishments in other cities and previews of what to expect in Aurora. The paper also offered detailed descriptions of how railcars would carry the immense machines and instructed attendees not to bring horses to the park on flight days, lest they be startled by low-flying planes.

Two weeks before Aurora's events, one of the Wrights' pilots set world records when he soared 20 miles at an altitude of 3,500 feet in Montreal. The machine headed for Aurora was said to be even better. The Wrights' manager was confident it would set several world records while in town.

On July 1, the planes were hauled through downtown streets to Driving Park, the grandstand between North Lake Street and Pennsylvania Avenue. Spectators were kept one hundred feet away from the machine as workers prepared it for the flight.

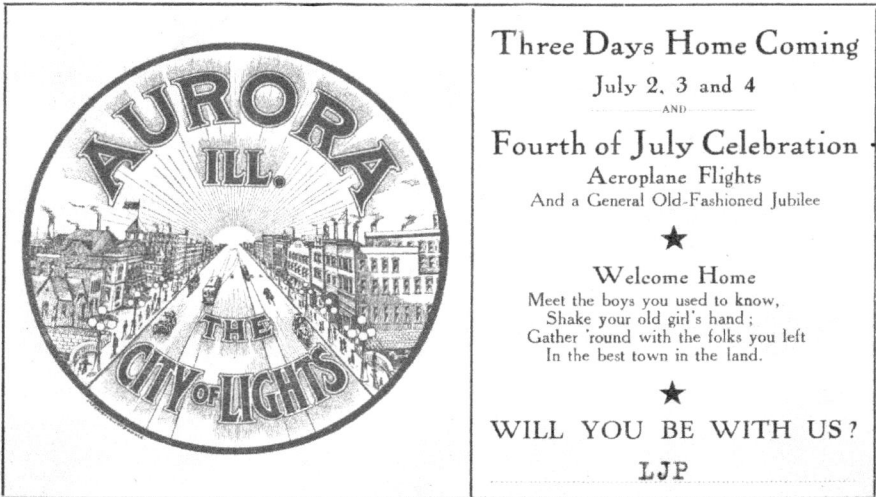

Postcard that advertised the Wright Brothers show on July 2–5, 1910. *From the collection of Tom Majewski.*

But because conditions were too windy, there were no flights on July 2 or July 4, 1910. Spectators were offered "wind checks"—free admission to the next day's flights. Businessmen worried.

"It is the policy of the Wright Brothers to deliver the goods, and we will make two more good flights in Aurora if we have to stay here a week to do it," the show's manager promised.

Now, on Tuesday, July 5, Welsh's flight was just twenty minutes old and in danger of an early end that might prompt a few coldhearted customers to demand refunds. City leaders might have been picturing the next day's headlines, which would undoubtedly become the city's permanent appendage: "Aurora, Illinois, the sight of that tragic airship crash."

200 feet...

The wind must have been rushing past Welsh's face. Pilots of Wright planes sat in a simple seat in front of the two propellers that moved the plane. There was no windshield or barrier in front of the pilot, just a few posts that stabilized the wings. The pilots were so exposed, it's possible the audience could see Welsh pulling at the lever as he began aiming for Mr. Henderson's oat field. Perhaps a few suspected by now that something had gone wrong.

For some people, airplanes were already a sign of a world turned upside down. Consider the other big event the rest of the nation was following on Independence Day that year: the boxing match between Jack Johnson, the first African-American heavyweight champion, and James J. Jeffries, the former champ. Jeffries was an American hero who had never lost. He had come out of retirement to demonstrate that the white race was king. (He would fail to prove that theory, losing in 15 rounds.) The country followed every detail of the fight. The *Beacon-News* set up a special wire service that would announce every punch thrown in Reno, Nevada, fifteen seconds after it landed. But the mayor of Aurora went to each theater in town and secured guarantees they would not show any footage of the fight, which had been deemed indecent and inflammatory.

Close-up of the propeller on the Wright airplane that flew in Aurora. *From the collection of the Aurora Historical Society.*

But progress, seemingly like Welsh's drop to Earth, would not be stopped. *100 feet...*

Finally, thirty-feet from the ground, the plane responded, either by Welsh shifting his weight or the gear unsticking. The plane came alive. It lurched up, clearing the roof of a house by a few feet.

Then the plane dove again.

Around 4:50 p.m., it crashed in the middle of Mr. Henderson's oat field.

In addition to finding a damaged plane in the middle of his field, Mr. Henderson had the misfortune of several hundred people trampling his crop to find out the fate of Al Welsh.

Several men look at the Wright airplane in 1910. *From the collection of the Aurora Historical Society.*

The news was good. Welsh had survived the flight, and so had the plane, except for a few broken posts.

So the day was not a total failure. Welsh was alive, the Wrights promised to pay for Mr. Henderson's oats and four days' gate receipts had finally collected enough to cover the Aurora business owners' costs. The Wrights' manager then promised one last free show on July 6.

It turned out to be worth the wait. Before a crowd of six thousand people, Welsh's plane was launched from Mr. Henderson's field. Like a giant, silvery bird, the plane made hawk-like swoops and powerful turns over the crowd. For fifty-five minutes, Welsh made the plane dance above Aurora, soaring over five hundred feet.

The crowd snapped pictures, trying to freeze the memory for anyone who might later doubt what they had seen.

After Welsh landed safely, he started his lowest altitude but most enthusiastic flight of the day, being carried off the field on the shoulders of the crowd

A man had flown in Aurora, making anything seem possible.

Casey at the Molar

Anyone attempting to write a true story about Casey Stengel should type with his fingers crossed, as absolution for accidental fabrications. Anyone attempting to explain how the future Hall of Fame manager saved his baseball career in Aurora, Illinois, should beg forgiveness for unintentional but inevitable misrepresentations.

Casey Stengel was not a liar; he was a storyteller. In his version of his life story, he was the buffoon, the hapless pawn of outside forces. His narratives circled the point, sometimes without reaching a destination. Then, at the end of his story, he'd wink. The deep wrinkles of his face would curl around his eye. All these theatrics distracted from the fact that Stengel was not a clown but a brilliant baseball mind.

These two sides must be reconciled to make sense of Stengel's time in Aurora. We can rely on statistics to tell the story of that season. In 1911, he led the Wisconsin-Illinois League with a .352 batting average, 148 hits and 50 stolen bases. He slugged five home runs (when that was a lot) and made 148 putouts in center field. We can look at those numbers and quite logically state that Stengel's performance in Aurora launched his career. It would be true and it would be boring. Casey Stengel was never dull.

It's more fun to tell it Stengel's way, with a gambling house, an umpire attack, a ridiculous contract negotiation and the train schedule that saved him from a career as a left-handed dentist. That's how Stengel told it, time after time: after fifty years in baseball, he dedicated nearly a dozen pages of his autobiography to the six months he spent in Aurora.

Here then is the story of Stengel's time in Aurora, as best as can be told without any intentional embellishment. He came ready to abandon baseball for a career in dentistry but found the magic that launched the greatest baseball managerial career of all time.

AURORA'S TEAM

In 1911, baseball was truly America's game. Ty Cobb and Honus Wagner were household names. A letter addressed simply to "Big Six" (nickname of Giants pitcher Christy Mathewson) could be delivered without further instruction. On the sports pages, only boxing and horse racing could grab column inches from baseball.

Although the heroes were well known, seeing a major league game was difficult, and hardly anyone had radios at home. Sixteen big league teams weren't nearly enough. More than any other time, fans quenched their baseball thirst by watching the local minor league squad. Even near Chicago, where the White Sox and Cubs were available, the collar counties were littered with clubs: Aurora, Joliet, Kankakee, Elgin, Rockford, Racine, Freeport and Osh Kosh all had minor league teams.

The hometown minor league team was a source of immense pride. Months before the first pitch was thrown, newspapers covered the local boys as thoroughly as a mayoral race. The first home game was practically a city holiday. For opening day of the 1910 season in Aurora, the two thousand employees of the railroad shops voted to close down so they could go to the game.

Despite this passion, there was little consistency in the minors. At the end of the season not all the teams had played the same number of games. Players left teams when they got a better offer from another team or the local mill. And it wasn't just players that left: leagues folded overnight when money ran out. Minor league teams sold tickets and stock but, to break even, they depended on selling their best players to major league teams, who mostly scouted by word of mouth.

Somehow heroes emerged from this chaos. Walter Johnson, the greatest right-handed pitcher of all time, was working at an Idaho telephone company and playing ball on the side when a scout noticed him. When Butts Wagner's minor league team needed another player, he suggested his little brother, a barber named Honus.

And so it was with hopes of uncovering a star that Aurora manager Al Tebeau went to visit his cousin George in April 1911. Tebeau was an Aurora original, comfortable in both high and low society. He was the esteemed manager of the baseball team and owner of the local brothel, saloon and gambling house. And when he was named manager, he loudly announced he was willing to spend money on good players.

Local fans needed the hope. The previous season had been a disaster. The 1910 Aurora Islanders had finished last in the Wisconsin-Illinois League, 33 ½ games out of first. Worse yet, they had been a financial and emotional disaster. The team had fallen behind so quickly, residents lost interest. Even in a city with more than 33,000 people, attendance at Fox River Park had slowed to a trickle.

City leaders rallied to revive the team. They brought in Tebeau, a former minor league catcher, to manage. They urged the community to buy stock and help raise the league's $500 entry fee. They even let residents choose the team's new name. Blues beat out Infants, Orioles, Foxes, Foxies, Wahoos and Doves. Tebeau outfitted the new club with sharp uniforms,

Young Casey Stengel in his Kansas City Red Sox uniform the season before he signed with Aurora. *Courtesy of the Baseball Hall of Fame.*

white shirts with navy blue collars with the name "Aurora" printed down the buttons.

Tebeau scoured the Midwest for players, even looking over his cousin's team in Missouri. As the cousins sat in the stands watching practice, Tebeau tried to buy a few contracts.

"I like that kid out in centerfield," Tebeau said, pointing to a fast, scrawny kid with a big nose and ears that stuck out. The year before, the kid had batted an unimpressive .236. He was raw and undisciplined and had fought a teammate in a funeral parlor.

"Take him with you," George told his cousin. "He doesn't look like much here."

And like that, Charley Stengel was headed for Aurora.

Hot Hitting, Hot Temper

After his first year in the minors, Charley Stengel had spent the off season between the 1910 and 1911 baseball seasons terrorizing both the living and dead patients of Western Dental College. In high school, he'd been a star football and baseball player. After winning the state championship, he was signed by the Kansas City minor league squad for $135 a month—a princely sum for a nineteen-year-old without a high school diploma.

In his first year, Stengel bounced among four teams. The switch from high school pitcher to minor league outfielder was humbling. Although he had great speed, Stengel struggled to judge fly balls. He had power at the plate but no discipline. After the season, it probably wasn't shocking when Stengel's father suggested he work on a back-up plan. Louis Stengel suggested dental school.

Later, when Stengel would tell stories of his youth, the only place that rivaled the chaos he created in Aurora was Western Dental School. For the rest of his life, Stengel loved to detail his difficulties as a left-handed dentist with right-handed tools. He relished the opportunity to tell about the time he stuck a cigar in a corpse's mouth or borrowed a dissected finger to give a friend a six-digit handshake.

Like most things, Stengel joked about dentistry, but he was privately serious. He wanted baseball to pay his way through school. So when he heard he had been signed by the Aurora Blues, Stengel, the boy who had batted .236 the year before, held out for a raise. He wanted $200 a month. The team offered $150 and no more. Stengel said he'd stick to cadaver extractions unless Aurora could pay $175, which was 12 percent of the team's total salary.

After two weeks of negotiations, Stengel won. But his arrival generated few news waves. The local paper made a small mention of a new outfielder named "Strengle." He was a last-minute addition, signed one week before opening day, another face in a crowd full of promising youngsters.

But Stengel quickly made his name known. In his first exhibition game, the newest Blue hit a home run that cleared the right field wall, which was rare. By opening day, the city was ready to believe in the Blues. More than 2,600 people, the second largest crowd in the city's history, were on hand. Sixty-five cars paraded the home team to their field, and the mayor's young son threw out the first pitch. The Blues fell in thirteen innings through no fault of their new center fielder. Stengel had two doubles, two putouts and an assist.

Something had clicked for Stengel. (Perhaps it was the prospect of staring at molars for the next fifty years.) He hit safely in 12 of the Blues' first 14 games, stole six bases and won 144 packages of Bull Durham tobacco for hitting two home runs.

By Game 14, the Blues had a respectable record of eight wins and six losses, which was good for fourth place. It was as high as they would rise all season. And the problems were not just on the field. By the beginning of June, just one month into the season, rainouts had cost the team $800 and

The 1911 Aurora Blues. Casey Stengel is in the bottom row, second from the right. Manager Al Tebeau is in the bottom row in the center. *From the collection of the Aurora Historical Society.*

put them in danger of not making payroll. More often than not, Stengel's name was in the paper for an outstanding catch, a great hustle on an infield hit or a heads up dash to score the winning run. But while his skills were sharpening, his maturity was still questionable at best.

On June 1, the Blues had to forfeit to the Rockford Wolverines. After being called out on strikes a third time, the ump laughed at Stengel, the supposed big shot. As the next batter got ready, Stengel snuck back to home plate with a bat and swatted the umpire in the butt. The result was a forfeit for the Blues, as well as an ejection and a $50 fine for Stengel.

When Stengel told the story later, he claimed that he convinced management to give him an advance on his paycheck before news of the fine came from league offices. "Everybody's sick at our house. I have to have money to pay up our bills, and I have to go to dental school," he pleaded. When the league showed up to deduct his fine, there was no check to deduct from, Stengel would say with a wink.

What he never added was this: the forfeit started a devastating losing streak for the Blues. For the next week, the team booted every crucial ground ball and struck out in every big at-bat. After losing nine games in a row, they were in last place. For all his undeniable brilliance, Stengel couldn't seem to stay out of trouble. And it was costing his team.

The Long Season

By July, the Wisconsin-Illinois league was showing signs of instability. The Osh Kosh Indians were not expected to last the season, and the last place Fond du lac Mudhens were actively trying to quit. In Aurora, fans rushed the field twice in a game against Madison, protesting close calls. The pressure for gate receipts was significant and teams scheduled exhibitions for gaps in the schedule. In late July, the Blues played an exhibition against the Negro League American Giants and their star pitcher, Rube Foster, putting two future Hall of Famers on Aurora's field.

On July 1, Stengel was hitting .341, which was good enough for fourth in the league. The local fans loved him, calling him "Happy Dutch" or "Pepper." Stengel would take the train to Cubs or Sox games; the big leagues must have seemed closer than ever. He even seemed to be growing into his new role as a team leader. When opponents mockingly called him "Ty" (sarcastically comparing him to Ty Cobb) and jeered him from the stands, Stengel simply belted a home run. No fight ensued.

By July 29, Aurora was in last place. Saying he could no longer abide by the conditions of the league, manager Al Tebeau quit. Perhaps it was just his star power, but one of the names that floated to fill in the rest of the season was that of the formerly hot-headed Stengel. The idea that a man who had hit an umpire with a bat earlier in the season could lead a team marked a significant shift. Stengel didn't get the job, but he was about to get the break of his life from a train schedule.

Larry Sutton wandered the country, watching local baseball players and sending written reports back to his employer, the Brooklyn Dodgers. At the time, scouts were a novelty. Many teams signed players on an owner's hunch. But the Giants and Dodgers had begun to see the value of trained eyes looking for talent. And so, Sutton ended up in Chicago on August 3, 1911, with nothing to do for a few hours between trains. Although Sutton scouted mostly high minor league teams, he had heard about Stengel and knew Aurora was only a short ride from the city.

By then, the Blues were hot. After Tebeau quit, the team won twenty of twenty-eight games and finally got out of the cellar. In a league where only

Casey Stengel in his Brooklyn Dodgers uniform, not long after his fateful season in Aurora. *Library of Congress.*

ten players had a batting average above .300, Stengel was on his way to finishing the year at a league-best of .352.

That day, word spread quickly that a major league scout was in the stands. Aurora played lights out, beating Green Bay 6–5. Stengel would later tell his audience that Sutton drafted him on superstition (Sutton liked players with light colored hair, Stengel said). Stengel didn't mention that he beat out three infield hits, stole two bases and made three putouts.

Based on Sutton's visit, the Dodgers bought the contracts of Stengel and Aurora pitcher Len Madden. (Madden went on to play six games in the major leagues.) The Blues were paid $1,000 for the pair.

Incredibly, a little more than a year later, Stengel, then known forever as "Casey," would be in the major leagues, going 4 for 4 in his debut. Within a decade, he'd be a World Series star, hitting two runs in a losing effort against Babe Ruth's Yankees.

And maybe none of it would have happened if Stengel hadn't ended up in Aurora, a simple train ride away from Chicago, close enough for a curious scout with spare time to drop in on a game, then file the quintessential report on Stengel. "Good hands, good power, runs exceptionally," Sutton wrote to the Dodgers. "Nice glove, left-handed line drive hitter. Good throwing arm. May be too damn aggressive, bad temper."

Extra Innings

In June 1963, at New York's Polo Grounds Stadium, Casey Stengel was holding court. He was no longer the wild youngster. He was the greatest manager of all time—a ten-time world champion—and the reigning storytelling master. By then, the Wisconsin-Illinois league was barely a memory; it had folded in 1915. (Aurora finished next to last the year after Stengel left and then dropped out.)

On the bench in front of Stengel was a row of Hall of Famers: Cardinals great Frankie Frisch razzed former Brooklyn outfielder seventy-five-year-old Zack Wheat; the great screwball pitcher Carl Hubbell, now sixty years old, complained about his elbow; right fielder Sam Rice, seventy-one, tried to remember everyone's name.

The men were in uniform for an old timers' game scheduled later that day, but they wanted to talk baseball, not play it. Their jokes were old enough to vote, and their stories had circled the bases many times.

Sitting among some of the game's giants, Stengel, at seventy-three, didn't talk about his World Series titles. Instead, in his own meandering Stengel way, he told the story about the time that he very nearly quit baseball for dentistry.

"I was down at Aurora, Illinois, and I went to this gambling house out there," Stengel said. "The guy who owned the place said to me: do you want to be a gambler or a ballplayer? You can make the big leagues as a player, but you're too stupid with cards to make it as a gambler. So I got out of there and do you know I didn't play cards for ten years and I hardly do today."

How does one make sense of Casey Stengel's career? How does a player go from being an unwanted minor leaguer to a pro player in less than two years? Did Stengel almost quit baseball to become a dentist? Was he really *that* close to tossing his career away?

Stengel did return to dental school one more off-season, but his heart wasn't in it and he never graduated. He was a baseball man and, although it's hard to separate the truth from perception with Stengel, the season in Aurora seemed pivotal, at least in his mind.

"If I hadn't made it to the majors fairly quickly, I probably would have become a dentist," said Stengel. "I was pretty good on extractions but not so hot on bridges."

Stengel's unofficial statistics from his 1911 season with the Aurora Blues: .352 batting average, 148 hits, 420 at-bats, 76 runs scored, 229 putouts, 27 assists, 8 errors, 22 doubles, 6 triples, 5 home runs and 50 steals. Led the league in average, hits and steals.

In the Line of Duty

*A*bout *12:25 a.m. Tuesday, October 29, 1918*
Gus Cordogan was adamant. No. More. Sugar.

No matter how much these two guys swore, no matter what sort of fuss they created, waiter Gus Cordogan was not giving them another ounce.

Gus had no way of knowing his patriotic resolve would lead to murder.

Standing in the diner on Broadway, he was the last line of defense against the government's restriction limiting each coffee drinker to two lumps and no more.

Without a doubt, these two jerks at the counter weren't going to change Gus's mind. Didn't we just finish a war? Weren't we all supposed to pitch in?

The loudmouth sitting on the third stool had an unforgettable face, one full of pockmarks, with a prominent nose and big ears. His friend, an ordinary-looking fellow around thirty-five years old, wore a dark brown velour derby that nearly covered his eyes but didn't hide his distinct jaw or thick blond hair.

Gus likely didn't know the two belligerent customers were practically royalty in the world of crime. They were wanted by Chicago police for their alleged involvement in half a dozen murders, at least two daring jewelry heists and the attempted murder of a Chicago detective.

Sitting on the other side of the diner, Aurora police sergeant Daniel Drake didn't know any of that criminal history either. So maybe it was their obnoxious attitude or the late hour that set off Drake's internal alarms. Perhaps it was just old-fashioned police instincts that told Drake there was more to this disturbance than an argument about the flavor of a beverage.

Postcard showing the corner of Fox and Broadway, where Walter Stevens and William von Gundy demanded more sugar in their coffee. *From the Tom Majewski collection.*

Drake made his way to the corner of Fox and Broadway and found a police box, the officer's only line of communication with headquarters. The boxes were posted throughout downtown and officers checked in every half hour.

Drake called Fred Hess, the detective at the desk.

While keeping an eye on the argument, Drake read out the license plate number of the Buick the two rowdies had driven.

"9-9-2-2-4," Drake told Hess.

Hess looked it up in the state's automobile register. The license came back as belonging to William von Gundy. But there was a problem: 99224 was supposed to be attached to a Ford, not a Buick.

An argument over sugar had just become an auto-theft case.

While in the army, Drake had won medals for sharpshooting. But he had also lost his leg, so he was forced to use crutches now. Drake couldn't handle these two guys by himself if they decided to bolt.

It was time to call the Swede.

Around 12:45 a.m. Tuesday, October 29, 1918

Alfred Olin, thirty-one, was one of the Aurora police department's stars.

Chief C.S. McCarty called him fearless, dependable and an excellent judge of people. And around police headquarters, he was known as the

42

Only known photo of Alfred Olin. *Courtesy of the Aurora Police Department.*

"Swede," even though his family had left Europe when he was three. While in his early twenties, Olin had worked at Western Wheel Scrapworks, where his size (he was more than six feet tall with a hefty frame) was an advantage to a laborer.

In 1911, Olin put his heft to another use by joining the Aurora Police Department. Photos of Aurora police in the early part of the twentieth century show row after row of burly mustached men, ready to use their bulk if necessary. Although he lacked the facial hair (he was cleanshaven under his bulbous nose), Olin fit right in, quickly moving up through the ranks of the force and earning a good reputation with both the command staff and the public.

As custom, people invited a police officer to their wedding for luck. Olin was often the officer asked to appear at these ceremonies because, according to Chief McCarty, he had a reputation for being of "gentlemanly manner and generally clean appearance."

Olin drove the department's patrol wagon and, after seven years on the force, he would occasionally fill in for detectives who were absent. The chief had even entrusted him with a new recruit, Lester Wedemaier, who had been in Aurora for less than a week after transferring from Hinckley.

With all his experience and expertise, Olin's comment before he left his home on Clark Street caught the attention of his wife and brother-in-law, who were sitting with him.

"I wouldn't go in to work tonight if they weren't short of men," Olin said.

Only minutes earlier, Olin had been called to headquarters to assist in a possible car-theft case.

Olin's wife watched as he struggled to get on his overcoat. Then, just before leaving, Olin added, "I feel that something is going to happen to me tonight."

Perhaps he said something like it a dozen times before on other police calls where nothing went wrong. But later, reflecting on what happened, Olin's family would have to wonder if the Swede had had a premonition as he walked out the door.

Nearly 1:00 a.m., Tuesday, October 29, 1918

The story wasn't making much sense to Alfred Olin.

These two guys were driving a stolen Buick, or at least a Buick with stolen plates, but they didn't seem too concerned. They told Olin they were driving from Dundee to Chicago but had ended up in Aurora. It would have been a detour the length of Kane County.

Olin and his partner, rookie cop Lester Wedemaier, had been sent to check out the situation.

"You will have to go over to headquarters with us," Olin said, when he approached the men.

"Is this about the sugar?" asked the man with the scarred face.

"That is one reason," Olin said, "and the other is that we want to look you over."

The name of the scarred-faced man was Frank Williams, although police knew him as William von Gundy. A month ago, he had been arrested by Chicago police with safe-cracking tools in his hand, tools police believed he had used in the dramatic robbery of Chicago's Heller-Rose Jewelry store three months earlier.

And yet compared to his partner, Von Gundy was a choirboy.

With neat blond hair and a charming manner, few would guess that Walter Stevens was one of Illinois's most arrogant and dangerous criminals.

He first made the newspapers as a "slugger" for a pipe-fitters union. As labor unions started to emerge in the United States, companies hired street gangs to discourage union activity. In response, the unions hired sluggers for protection and recruitment. Stevens was a natural fit, adept at carefully explaining (with fists if necessary) how important unions were. And for the really stubborn ones, Stevens simply used a bullet.

Stevens also had a reputation as the immune gunman. He bragged openly that he had been arrested more than three hundred times and never so much as paid a fine. In fact, while he and Von Gundy were sitting in the Aurora diner, they were wanted by police for their involvement in the Heller-Rose robbery. During the escape, Stevens had nearly killed a Chicago officer, trying to crush him between two cars while fleeing the scene.

In 1918, police departments had no method for seeing who was wanted in other jurisdictions. A possible stolen car was all the information Olin and Wedemaier had at their disposal when they approached Stevens and Von Gundy and asked them to get in the Buick.

If he suspected anything more serious, Olin didn't take the time to search either Von Gundy or Olin. It would be a fatal mistake.

So Chicago's underworld leaders got in the front seat of the Buick while Olin and Wedemaier got in the back.

From the back seat, Olin narrated directions to the police station as Von Gundy drove: turn at the corner, west on Fox Street toward the police station.

Finally, Olin asked Von Gundy to make a left into the driveway of the police station.

"Like hell I will," Von Gundy responded, speeding past city hall.

Just after 1 a.m. Tuesday, October 29, 1918
October 29 was officially the start of Lester Wedemaier's third week as an Aurora police officer.

The twenty-three-year-old, rosy-cheeked baseball fan had left the Hinckley police force precisely twenty-two days earlier. In Aurora, he replaced an officer only recorded in the historical annals as "Ugland," whose tenure with Aurora lasted only four days.

As the car driven by a suspected car thief sped away down Benton Street, Wedemaier might have been thinking that Ugland had the right idea.

As William von Gundy accelerated past headquarters, Walter Stevens—described in Chicago papers as "noted bad man with a trigger"—pointed a gun at the Aurora officers.

Stevens fired, hitting Olin twice in the chest.

"They got me," Olin groaned.

The shots must have exploded through the car but, later, Wedemaier would hardly remember hearing them.

Wedemaier, six feet tall and 204 pounds, grabbed at the gun. Stevens fired a third shot over Wedemaier's shoulder that went through the roof and ricocheted through the plate glass window of Harkison Drug Store.

Wedemaier finally got a hand on the gun, but Stevens kept firing. His fourth bullet hit Wedemaier in the groin. Stevens had been in gunfights before and, when Wedemaier grabbed his leg after being shot, Stevens saw an opportunity. He shoved Wedemaier out of the car's passenger side door, and the policeman tumbled onto the street, falling on his hip.

Lying on Downer Street, Wedemaier grabbed for his gun. Stevens shot once more out the window. Wedemaier tried to return fire. His gun jammed. He stood up and attempted to get behind the car, which had stopped on the Fox River Bridge, but his revolver still wouldn't fire. That's when Wedemaier heard another blast from inside the Buick and Olin fell out of the car.

The Buick began to flee. Wedemaier watched as Olin raised himself up on his elbow and fired four shots. Bleeding, Wedemaier tried to find a taxi to chase the shooters.

Olin told Wedemaier to run to the station for help. The Buick was already gone.

3:00 p.m. October 29, 1918

When Alfred Olin arrived at St. Joseph's Hospital, the doctors could barely detect his pulse.

"He was as near to dead, without dying, as any person could be," Dr. Sherman told the *Beacon-News*.

Sherman gave Olin some stimulants, and that revived him a bit. One of the shots had hit Olin in the chest, one inch below his left nipple. The bullet went straight through his chest, pierced his lung and grazed the outer edge of his heart. Doctors couldn't reach it. A second bullet went in to the right of his abdomen, traveled eight inches through his body and then popped out at his hip.

Although Wedemaier had also been seriously wounded, he managed to run to the police headquarters.

The same day Olin and Wedemaier were shot, Sergeant Daniel Drake, the officer who made the original police call, went to Chicago to look through "the rogue's gallery," the photos of wanted criminals. Drake immediately spotted a man with a scarred face and a man with thick blond hair and a pronounced jaw.

Officers from across the state spread out with orders to shoot to kill. A hired man found Olin's hat, the metal piece indicating badge No. 105 still attached, in an oat field three miles south of Little Rock, Illinois.

The stolen Buick was found in western Kendall County. Inside, police found pipe wrenches, burglary tools and a 1918 Ohio license tag. There were also seven bullet holes in the car, including one on the roof, the shot that just missed Wedemaier's head.

But by late afternoon, twelve hours after the gun battle, Olin's stomach started to hemorrhage.

"He cannot recover," Dr. Sherman said.

At 3:15 p.m. Alfred Olin became the first Aurora officer in the department's sixty-one-year history to die in the line of duty. It would be another five years before either of the shooters would spend a day in prison.

June 11, 1919, Geneva

The trial of Walter Stevens was a media sensation. Even as The Great War wound down, news of his trial ran side by side with "Austria quits" on the front page of the *Beacon-News*.

Wanted for the murder of Olin, the attempted murders of two other police officers and several bank robberies, Stevens had managed to elude police for five months. Then, on February 8, 1919, Stevens strolled into the Kane County State Attorney Office and turned himself in.

"I just got tired of being hounded by police," he told the *Chicago Tribune*. "They tried to kill me because I knew too much. I've been in Chicago all the time and the police knew it."

Although he was facing the death penalty for Olin's murder, Stevens seemed to hardly break a sweat. Despite his extensive criminal history (it was said that hardly a daring crime in the city was committed without Stevens ending up at the top of the suspect list), he enjoyed mysterious connections that kept him out of prison for fifty-one years.

And on June 11, when his trial started in the Kane County Courthouse in Geneva, Stevens had full confidence that his team of lawyers (which initially included an aggressive attorney from Chicago named Clarence Darrow) would free him again.

He smiled at people who identified him as Olin's killer.

"I always feel great 24 hours every day," Stevens told a reporter who asked how he was feeling.

Kane County State Attorney Charles Abbott and defense attorney W.W. O'Brien opened the trial with a flourish, outlining their case and accusing each other of jury tampering. Abbott was confident, but O'Brien was holding a hidden ace in the trial, a ruse that had taken months to prepare. A few months before Stevens turned himself, an odd but friendly salesman calling himself A.H. Byrnes had shown up in Aurora. Wearing sunglasses, Byrnes handed out cigars and made sure to introduce himself to plenty of police officers.

Byrnes made a point of asking patrol officer Lester Wedemaier for directions to the Hotel Bishop. Wedemaier didn't recognize that the lost tourist behind the sunglasses was really Walter Stevens. Prosecutors proved the X-rays Stevens had used as his alibi (he claimed to be hospitalized when Olin was shot) were from the wrong leg. But the sunglasses stunt was too much to overcome.

"Stevens had men testify for him in this case that have sworn him off the gallows before," prosecutors Harvey Gunsul bellowed in the closing arguments. "If he is innocent, why was it necessary to go to Aurora to continue framing his alibi?"

It was no use. After three ballots, Stevens was acquitted of Olin's murder. Stevens had enough time to shake hands with every juror before he was immediately rearrested for the shooting of Wedemaier.

At that trial, prosecutors were ready for the defense.

On April 10, 1920, the same man who was found not guilty of shooting Alfred Olin was convicted of the attempted murder of Wedemaier. For the first time in his life Walter Stevens, the immune gunman, was going to jail.

Or so it seemed.

With the help of state senators who testified on his behalf, Stevens appealed the case all the way to the U.S. Supreme Court. Meanwhile, he also skipped out on his bail, fled to Florida and was involved in two more murders.

At the same time, William von Gundy was finally arrested for a North Carolina bank robbery. He later escaped in dramatic fashion, killing the local police chief.

In Illinois, Governor Len Small tried to grant Stevens a pardon, but to no avail. Finally, on October 29, 1923, Stevens, at age fifty-six, was sent to Joliet.

"I suppose I'll lose all my identity now," he said. "I'll not be known as Walter Stevens, merchant, but by some number like 3222."

He spent less than two years in jail.

"In jail at 56, he's an old man whom all the guns and all the revenge in the world can't make young again," described the *Beacon-News* in an editorial. "Walter Stevens is broke. They broke him when they broke his pride." By the time those words were written, the Aurora Police Department had already felt the sting of losing another officer to violence.

10:15 p.m. Sunday, April 15, 1928

It had been, for the most part, an uneventful Sunday shift behind the desk for Sergeant Clinton Dickerson.

Dickerson had missed the night's only excitement—if you could call it that—while he was eating dinner. When he returned from his meal, Patrol Officer Thompson Richardson had filled him in on the highlights. Early in the evening, former East Aurora wrestling coach Bill Robinson had been in a crash with two kids who fled the scene. Richardson had hardly finished taking the report, when Mr. C.A. Howell came in to report that a Chrysler roadster had been stolen from in front of his house on Iowa Avenue.

Police figured the two incidents might be connected, so Richardson and patrolman Harry Montgomery were dispatched to look for these kids.

It would probably turn out to be nothing more than two isolated pranks, but Dickerson was edgy. A few minutes earlier, he could have sworn he heard three gunshots coming from downtown. But when he looked outside, everything appeared to be normal. People were going about their business, shopping and eating in downtown Aurora. No one seemed to have heard these phantom shots. Dickerson went back to his desk work.

A few minutes later, Officer Richardson staggered through the police station doors with a teenager. Richardson was crouched over, one hand over his stomach.

He was using his other hand to stick his gun in the teenager's back.

Both Richardson and the teen were bleeding; their faces were deathly white.

"This punk got me," Richardson growled and then swayed. Then both he and the long-faced teen collapsed in the lobby.

8:00 p.m. Sunday, April 15, 1928

Delmar Miller and Francis Houston were hardly criminal masterminds. Although they were barely old enough to drive, they were already on their way to substantial juvenile records.

Miller, seventeen years old, was lanky, and his hair bounced up in a cowlick that seemed to accentuate his generally overwhelmed and blank expression. Miller was born in downstate Bloomington, but he became familiar with the Fox Valley after he served a term at the St. Charles School for Boys for stealing a Ford with a friend, nineteen-year-old Francis Houston. Houston, who worked with his father as an apprentice mechanic on the railroad, was also sent to the St. Charles School.

Francis Houston's prison photo. *Courtesy of the Aurora Police Department.*

Miller bloomed in St. Charles, starring on the school's basketball team and serving as an aide for the teachers. But when he returned to Bloomington, the boys returned to their old ways.

For reasons lost to history, they decided, in mid-April, to grab a gun, steal a Nash Coupe and head north. Around 8 p.m., while passing through Aurora, the Coupe got a flat tire and the boys, apparently without any useful knowledge of cars, decided to steal a replacement. They spotted a Chrysler roadster parked at 123 Iowa Avenue. It was an easy steal.

But while fleeing the scene, the boys hit William Robinson's vehicle and cracked the bumper. As soon as Robinson got out of his car, the wrestling coach pegged these kids as troublemakers. Seeing the age of the kids and the fancy car they were driving, he suspected they might have stolen the car. Robinson told the boys, under the guise of reporting the damage to the bumper, he would need to talk to police. He asked them to follow him to the station downtown. The boys followed him to the city limits, then took off on a side street.

But Robinson continued on to police headquarters, figuring he should tell the police about the boys. When Robinson got to the station, he spoke to the officer who was filling in for another patrolman during his lunch break, Thompson Richardson.

In the Line of Duty

Around 9:00 p.m., Sunday, April 15, 1928

In the early 1920s, an Aurora policeman had to be a jack-of-all-trades, equally adept at sniffing out craps games on La Salle Street, solving homicides and occasionally, at least in one instance, dealing with an explosive goat.

Richardson, however, was facing what seemed to be more typical police work, albeit one that still required a tactful response: two boys had hit a car, then fled before they could report it to police.

After taking the report, Richardson, age thirty-seven, went to look for the Chrysler, which he believed had been stolen from Iowa Avenue the same night.

Richardson had been on the police force for almost seven years, following a career as a brakeman on the railroad and a short stint with the fire department. He was a pleasant man, and his disposition seemed to match the gentlemanly bow tie in the Aurora uniform.

He and his wife Edda had three children: Evelyn, age sixteen; Ralph, thirteen; and Virginia, three. Richardson would sometimes let his oldest daughter ride in the sidecar of the department's motorcycle, nearly tipping as they rounded the city's corners.

"Some policemen, when they get to be policemen, they think 'I am somebody,'" Evelyn remembered. "My dad wasn't at all like that."

His easy disposition allowed him to handle a job where the daily duties could range from bombastic animals on a Thursday to following two young boys in a stolen car on a Sunday evening.

Around 9:00 p.m., Richardson spotted his two young suspects driving the Chrysler near Lake and Downer Streets. He and his partner followed the car along Jericho Road, but the Chrysler got away.

Richardson finally stopped at a police box to call into headquarters. The desk had an update: the Chrysler had been spotted by its owner, parked in front of the downtown post office. Richardson drove to the spot and, sure enough, the Chrysler was sitting on Stolp Avenue. The door was open, no one was inside and the keys were dangling from the ignition. Richardson, suspecting the boys would be back, put the transmission in lock and then ducked into the vestibule of the post office.

He'd wait them out.

10:00 p.m., Sunday, April 15, 1928

Twenty minutes passed before Miller and Houston returned. As soon as they got in the car, Richardson sprung out of his hiding spot, appearing at the door with his gun drawn. The fun was over. They were going to headquarters.

As the boys got out of the Chrysler, Miller kept his hand in the left pocket of his overcoat. Richardson immediately checked the pocket but found nothing.

He grabbed both teens—Miller on his left side, Houston on his right—and started the two-block march to headquarters. The boys looked harmless. Houston, who had stolen cars before, tried to be cocky, but it was mostly teenage bluffing. Miller was a goofy-looking kid with a long face, looking more like a bookworm than bandit.

But the car theft was more than a youthful prank, and Richardson had missed something during his search. Miller had a small .25 caliber pistol tucked in his right pocket. And before Richardson had grabbed the boys, Houston had encouraged Miller to use it.

A few steps into their march down Fox Street, Houston suddenly motioned to Miller.

"Do your stuff," Houston growled.

Miller threw his coat on the officer and fired once through his pocket. The bullet hit Richardson in his stomach, moving through his intestines.

Both boys jerked away. As Richardson reached for his gun, they ran east.

Thompson Richardson. *Courtesy of the Aurora Police Department.*

"By God, he shot me," Richardson thought as he watched Miller run. "I'm going to give him plenty."

In the heart of downtown, Richardson fired twice. Both bullets hit Miller in the back, passing straight through his body. Richardson kept advancing, and Miller started to fall, but the officer grabbed him, shoving a gun in his back. Bleeding from the stomach and without backup, Richardson marched the boy toward headquarters, about two blocks away.

Houston, meanwhile, ran toward Water Street unscathed. Hundreds of people standing on the streets heard shots fired and saw the boy running.

No one tried to stop him.

Tuesday, April 17, 1928

Delmar Miller confessed before he even left the hospital.

The seventeen-year-old admitted to former Aurora police chief Frank Michels that he had shot Richardson. But Miller was also quick to put the blame on his fellow car thief, Francis Houston.

"We were walking around the corner," Miller told Michels from his hospital bed. "And Houston motioned to me—you better shoot, only chance to get away—that's what he meant when he motioned. I shot through the pocket."

After thirty years as chief, Michels retired the day Richardson was shot. But the chief who had solved some of Illinois's biggest cases returned to handle one more murder case.

"Even though you knew this man was going to die," Michels pressed, "you wouldn't want to change that statement?"

"The one thing I want to say is that I was sorry after I shot him," Miller said.

Meanwhile, in the same St. Charles hospital, Richardson was clinging to life. His pulse had slowed with every passing day. Doctors, who were at first optimistic, began to see that the bullet had done too much damage.

At 1:35 p.m., three days after he was shot on the streets of downtown Aurora, Thompson Richardson died.

As if startled from a cozy nap, the citizens of Aurora who had stood by as Richardson had a gunfight with Miller and Houston—men and women who had watched Houston flee the scene—suddenly grieved for their hero. The *Beacon-News* started the "Richardson Fund" to raise money for the officer's wife and three children. Average citizens, suddenly remembering the protection they took for granted, gave generously.

The St. Olaf Church choir donated $10 while the Police Benevolent Association gave $500. North Aurora mayor Charles Greene chipped in $10, while the Greenman Elementary schoolboy patrol scrounged up $1.05

for their idol. By the end of the month, more than $3,300 had been raised. The donations would eventually pay off the family's $4,700 mortgage, allowing his widow, Edda Richardson, to live in her Spencer Street home into her nineties.

On the day of Richardson's funeral, residents filled the streets of Aurora. A brigade of fifteen city, county and state motorcycles led the procession to Riverside Cemetery. City officials, firefighters and the police department leadership walked in front of three cars filled with floral offerings.

To lead the procession, the department selected perhaps the only officer who could match Richardson's bravery—a veteran officer, who had been in the car when Alfred Olin was shot, who chased the murderers' car even as he bled through his uniform.

Lester Wedemaier would lead the funeral procession.

Friday, April 20, 1928

A few blocks from where they had stood by as Richardson was shot, citizens of Aurora now came to pay tribute.

Unable to find seats, more than a thousand people stood silently outside St. Olaf Church for two hours. Inside, Reverend Oscar Johnson stood at the altar of his church. He had been at the hospital with Richardson as he faded away.

"I stand before you to pay tribute to a man of valor," Johnson began his sermon. "A man, in time of the greatest danger, who thought not of his own deadly injury but whose thoughts were on fulfilling his duty. When mortally wounded and falling upon the street, his heroism was amplified, his courageous instinct enabled him to bring in his man and complete the task assigned to him. He apprehended a murderer."

Johnson also spoke of the two boys who had been involved in Richardson's death. They were not brilliant criminals. They were two reckless, stupid kids.

"It is the God-given duty of every parent to raise their children to hate lawlessness and to love that which is right, that which is good, that which is eternal, that which is holy and sacred," Johnson bellowed from the pulpit. "Every one of you are examples. Someone is observing you and walking in your footsteps. God pity you if you are not an example for good."

Miller and Houston would eventually pay the price for their lawlessness.

After walking, hitching and stowing away on trains, Houston made it home to Bloomington, where the police were waiting on his front porch. He would later be convicted of auto theft and spend less than four years in jail. Miller, the shooter, recovered from his injuries and pleaded guilty to murder. He received a life sentence. In 1948, Miller was one of twelve Illinois inmates who volunteered for a wartime experiment, in which he was injected with malaria fever in exchange for having his sentence reduced to sixty years. He was paroled in 1955 at the age of forty-nine and died in Bloomington in 1986.

The prison sentence did not heal Aurora. Richardson's murder represented much more to the people who had crammed Reverend Johnson's church. The invincible shield of law enforcement had been damaged; the blanket of security, shredded.

It was up to Johnson to remind the crowd that death would not chill the work of Aurora police.

When Alfred Olin had been killed in 1918, the city survived. Now, facing another murder, Richardson's death was not a reason for panic but a reminder that no matter the danger, police would face it.

"I recall the reign of terror that many residents of our city experienced two years ago when home after home was entered by some burglar or band of burglars," Johnson told the congregation. "A resident sent in a call for police. Within three minutes, police protection was granted.

"We are here to honor the efficient police department of our city. We know them for making Aurora a safe place in which to live, to establish our homes, to raise our families. We honor them for the protection we are assured of, hovering around us.

"It is the duty of every good citizen to make his life an example for good. The hero of the day calls you to fulfill that duty regardless of cost."

On the Trail of a Killer

For a little while, on a pleasant Saturday afternoon, Aurora stared into the heavens.

At about noon on April 28, 1923, a plane wheeled and dipped over the city, spelling out a two-mile tall "L" in a trail of white smoke. From their front lawns, residents watched the plane buzz through an oversized "U" and curl through a massive "C."

Some Aurorans had probably heard about skywriting (first demonstrated in England the year before) but seeing words painted on the atmosphere must have been an astonishing and welcome diversion for a weary town.

By that time, Aurora was a city of deep contrasts. It was growing at an astounding rate, but the expansion was dogged by rumors that Aurora was a wild, lawless outpost.

The police chief estimated that in one thousand homes—over ten percent of the city—residents were brewing bootlegged liquor in their basements. Cops had confiscated so much moonshine that the illegal liquor was used in municipal vehicles to keep the radiators from freezing.

The booze attracted trouble.

Five years earlier, Chicago gangsters had murdered an Aurora police officer on downtown streets. In the previous nine years, three young Aurora women had been beaten to death. All the cases were unsolved, and Chicago papers were calling Aurora "the city of mysterious murders."

Labor unrest also cast a shadow. At the new Burlington Central Railroad Station, immigrants walked out over poor working conditions, and riots threatened to break out.

Any diversion was welcomed and, for a few minutes, Aurorans marveled as Captain Cyril Turner of England's Royal Air Force cut through the air at 100 miles per hour. When he spelled out "LUCKY STRIKE" in full, the trail stretched more than six miles, the largest message ever written in the sky.

Seeing the words, some railroad workers became so excited, they momentarily thought their strike was settled and the pilot had been hired to wish them luck. The stunt turned out to be nothing more than a fantastic advertising ploy by a tobacco company on a tour of one hundred American cities.

But as the city's attention was drawn toward heaven, down below on the West Side, perhaps beneath the giant "S" in the sky, the last details of a hideous plot were being worked out.

The horrifying plan was finalized in a humble, one-story house on Indian Trail. It would disgust and captivate residents and put the Fox Valley on the front page of newspapers across the country.

Solving this bizarre crime would change Aurora's reputation and make the town's police chief a law enforcement legend.

It all began to unfold at 6:00 p.m., the day after the skywriting show, when a tiny candle was extinguished in the City of Lights.

THE PECULIAR FLORIST

Edward was worried about his brother, Warren Lincoln.

Ever since Lincoln's wife and brother-in-law had mysteriously vanished in January, the forty-five-year-old Auroran claimed a man had been following him. The stranger, a well-dressed, sandy-haired man, had trailed Lincoln to the movies, lurked behind him while he shopped downtown and lingered outside the large greenhouse next to his home.

A few weeks before the skywriter's visit, Lincoln reported this stranger to police. He was convinced the man was trying to kill him and speculated it might be connected to the disappearance of his wife and her brother. Aurora Police Captain Fred Grass checked out the story, even assigning an officer to tail Lincoln, but police never saw anyone following him.

It was all so unsettling that Edward and his brother worked out a signal. Lincoln would light a candle in his window if everything was OK.

His story was odd, but Lincoln was a bit peculiar himself. At 5'6" and weighing 160 pounds, Lincoln's most prominent feature was his large, bald

Warren Lincoln. Beacon-News *archives.*

head and big eyes that made him look like a hawk. Still, he was friendly and likeable. Harmless even.

He wasn't shy about his relationship to the famous president. Warren Lincoln's great-great-grandfather and Abe Lincoln's great-grandfather were brothers. The connection was tenuous. However, when Warren Lincoln later became the focus of national media attention, few papers failed to mention the family lineage.

In 1912, Warren married a tall, severe woman named Lina Shoup and began to pursue a law degree. The law career didn't last. In 1918, he had a mental breakdown, an event that would lead him from Mount Pulaski to Aurora, the place of all his troubles.

To deal with his stress, Lincoln gravitated to horticulture and zeroed in on the fertile ground surrounding the Fox River. He bought twenty acres of land at 355 West Indian Trail and built a modest home with an impressive greenhouse. He became known for his gladiolus and sweet peas.

Still, the move to Aurora didn't ease his tension. Lincoln and Lina argued. Things only got worse when Lina's brother, Byron Shoup, moved in. Lincoln told police he and his wife's arguments escalated to violence. He claimed Byron had tried to poison him at least three times.

That, Lincoln told the cops, might explain the stranger, who began tailing him shortly after Lina and Byron disappeared. He told his sixteen-year-old housekeeper the stranger was an assassin sent by his wife. He decided to take precautions.

Each night, Lincoln put the candle in his window. But at 6:00 p.m. on April 29, the light went out. Edward rushed to his brother's house.

There was blood on the window. Papers were scattered everywhere. Lincoln was missing.

Aurora Police Chief Frank Michels was one of the first officers on the scene. As he walked up to Lincoln's house, he had no way of knowing it was the start of an investigation that would change his city.

THE BOY CHIEF

By 1923, Michels was known throughout Illinois for his tenacity as an investigator and his long tenure with the department.

Born at the corner of New York and Broadway to a hardworking farmer, Michels took his first job at age eleven, leading a blind Civil War veteran through the streets of Aurora. When he was twenty-

Chief Frank Michels in 1906. *Courtesy of the Aurora Police Department.*

one, Aurora police bought their first patrol wagon and needed someone to drive the horses. With his farm experience, Michels became an Aurora officer in June 1887. He quickly stood out for his ability to use his head. Not long after he was hired, Michels, working alone, tracked down a murderer by tracing a cheap watch found at the scene to a Chicago pawnshop.

Michels developed a reputation for working long hours and having no patience for politics. His brutal honesty clashed with some (including the mayor), but it won over many others, like the angry mob that gathered on North Broadway during a particularly nasty railroad strike. The mob looked ready to brawl before Michels leapt onto a car, lectured the crowd for fifteen minutes and convinced everyone to head home.

In 1898, at just thirty-three years old but with a chubby baby face that made him look much younger, Michels was named chief of police. After his promotion, the legend of "the boy chief" only grew. He remained actively involved in cases, including a few that would help cultivate the psychological tactics he would use on the Lincoln case. To the demanding residents of Aurora, however, Michels was only as good as his last arrest.

When he approached Lincoln's house in 1923, his luster had dulled. The horrifying, unsolved murders of three women had led the public to openly question their chief. Michels personally handled the investigations but was unable to get a conviction.

That failure undoubtedly still stung Michels when he arrived at Lincoln's home. Lincoln was a well-known man, and the police department would be closely watched. It didn't take long for Michels to realize that, even amid the chaos, there was something odd about the murder scene.

THE FIRST THEORY

The doors of the house were locked, but a window next to Lincoln's bed was wide open. Michels noticed blood spattered on the windowsill and a curtain near the bed. A pool of blood and a large club, perhaps the weapon used in the attack, were found on the floor of the greenhouse.

Near the home, Michels found a woman's heel print pushed deep into the mud. Down the dirt road, Lincoln's business papers were scattered for two hundred yards. Among the papers was a business card that read "Milo Durand, private detective." Was this the suspicious stranger who had been following Lincoln?

Along the road, patrolman Lester Wedemaier fished Lincoln's nightshirt and his sleeping cap out of a cistern. The clothes were torn and covered in blood. Wedemaier also found a woman's glove. Michels told the public he was looking to question Lina Lincoln, Byron Shoup and Milo Durand about Lincoln's murder. Police sent a bulletin out across the country.

Byron Shoup. Beacon-News *archives.*

"Lincoln was not killed in the house, of that we are sure," Michels told reporters. "He was hit over the head with the club while he slept."

The boy chief didn't tell the press that he already had his own theory, one that would prove his investigative skills were as sharp as ever. Aurora detectives photographed the scene and recorded evidence in notebooks. They noted that Lincoln's watch and sixty-seven cents had been left on the dresser. A half-eaten pie was left out on the kitchen table. Next to Lincoln's bed was a book, *Silent, White and Beautiful* by Tod Robbins. The story was about a French man who murdered his nagging wife and hid her body inside a plaster statue he kept in his house. Considering that it was found at a crime scene, the story added an extra chill.

Privately, Michels didn't believe the story the press had latched on to, that Lincoln had been murdered. The chief's theory gained traction when he received an odd letter typed in green ink from someone who claimed to have seen Lincoln commit suicide in Baltimore. Michels's gut said this letter was a lie, but he had little proof either way. He needed evidence.

He ordered the latest in blood analysis, what is called an "Abrams Test," a test based on the theory that everyone's blood has a unique vibration. Lab technicians poured blood into a bowl that had wires attached to it. Next, a person—the "controller"—held both ends of the wire as the blood was vibrated. The number of vibrations showed whether the blood was human and what sex it belonged to. The test ended when a second person tapped the controller's abdomen and heard a wooden, rather than clear, sound.

The test results showed the blood found on Lincoln's window belonged to a man who was eccentric and suffering from a disease. Despite the scientific nature of the test, it turned out to be dead wrong.

But the blood test results didn't matter to Michels. He was already on his way to Chicago. Michels had figured out what happened to Lincoln.

The murder victim was alive.

THE STRANGE STORY

Six weeks after Warren Lincoln disappeared, a letter from the supposed dead man was sent to his brother. Lincoln asked his brother to meet him in Room 86 of the Grace Hotel in downtown Chicago. Michels, Lincoln's brother, Kane County Sheriff W.E. Orr and *Beacon-News* reporter Wayne Miller headed for the hotel on June 12.

When they opened the door, Lincoln was sitting at the end of the bed in one of his old suits, sobbing. He appeared to have lost twenty pounds, and he nearly fainted when police walked in. Clearly, being dead had taken a toll on him.

Gradually, Lincoln steadied himself. Even the most suspicious officers must have been shocked to see the short, bald man again. But that wasn't the biggest surprise. Lincoln's explanation for his disappearance was a whopper.

"I had just dozed off," Lincoln began, remembering the day he vanished. "I heard a noise on the porch outside the window. It sounded like the rustling of a curtain. Just as I got up, a man stepped through the window."

Lincoln told officers he jumped out the window in his nightshirt, only to run into two more men who beat him unconscious. While the newspaper reporter carefully recorded the statement, Michels surveyed the room. He studied Lincoln, noting what he was wearing, how he was acting. The baby-faced chief listened quietly but skeptically.

Lincoln continued. When he awoke, his wife, Lina, who had vanished months earlier, and several other men were present. Lincoln was naked and blindfolded. Lina and the men forced Lincoln into a sedan, maybe a Chevrolet. They took him to Chicago, Lincoln said, and locked him in a basement room, where his captors gave him new clothes to wear.

"I was kept in that basement for three weeks and one day," Lincoln said. "I asked my wife several times what they were going to do, and she wouldn't tell me."

The story went on, with Lincoln adding spectacular details about his captivity. Finally, he explained his escape with gusto.

Lincoln said the captors eventually let him in on their plan. They were dope runners and wanted his help. Lincoln pretended to consider their offer but slipped away on a train and finally contacted his brother.

The room must have been silent when Lincoln finished his bizarre tale.

Michels wasn't fazed. He had been waiting for Lincoln to reappear and immediately started to poke holes in the tale.

"How did you get that old suit of yours?" Michels asked.

"My wife brought me that," Lincoln stammered.

Michels reached into Lincoln's suit pocket and pulled out the florist's pocketknife. If he was kidnapped and stripped, where did that come from? Lincoln assured the chief his wife had given him the knife too.

And what about the label on the bottom of Warren's shoe? How, Michels wanted to know, did he buy a shoe in Denver if he was trapped in Chicago?

"I won't answer any questions," Lincoln said. "I'm too nervous. I want to be left alone."

Warren Lincoln's home at 355 West Indian Trail. Beacon-News *archives.*

Two days later, Lincoln apparently regained his strength and was back in Aurora, working at his greenhouse. Outside his humble house, where the front porch was held up by cement blocks, the newspaper snapped pictures of neighbors happily shaking hands with the missing man.

On October 20, 1923, Lincoln dropped out of sight again. Neighbors casually shook their heads. He'll return, they said.

The media gleefully described Lincoln as the "eccentric horticulturist." But Aurora's normally press-friendly chief gave the newspapers no comment. He wasn't about to reveal his theory.

THE SURPRISING LETTER

The break in Aurora's most notorious murder did not come from the discovery of a weapon or a hidden fingerprint. It came from the ribbon of a typewriter.

In the weeks after Aurora florist Warren Lincoln disappeared and then reappeared six weeks later, Chief Frank Michels tried to make sense of Lincoln's bizarre alibi.

Michels never believed Lincoln was dead. In fact, he speculated Lincoln had probably murdered his wife and her brother. But there wasn't any evidence to back up the theory. It was all hunch and no bodies.

Then, after months without a word from Lina, her family received a letter that read, "Please send $500 to the Evanston post office. Tell no one."

The note was typed in green ink and matched a green personal ad, also sent by someone claiming to be Lina, submitted to the *Chicago Tribune* days after Lincoln was supposedly murdered, as well as a third green letter from an anonymous man who claimed he had seen Lincoln kill himself.

Michels looked at the letters. What did they add up to? Each piece was somewhat suspicious, but all three were a long way from evidence in a murder case. And in the meantime, Lincoln had vanished again.

Michels, who was about to leave for California on vacation, needed a different approach. He couldn't go after Lincoln for murder.

Lina's family sent the $500. Not long after that, another letter (and another request for money) showed up. This time, Lina's sister decided to meet her sister at the Evanston post office with the reply. Lina didn't show, but Warren Lincoln did. He escaped before anyone could catch him.

Michels had had enough. Lincoln would be charged with obtaining $500 under false pretenses. If they could find him.

THE FIVE CONFESSIONS

On Jan. 13, 1924, a short, bald man walked into the Charles Baumgarten Store in Chicago. The visitor was looking for a job as a calendar salesman. He had references, including that of Dr. E.C. Van Hook, from his hometown in Mount Pulaski.

It wasn't long before the company called Van Hook, and Van Hook called Aurora police, and police set out to a get a look at this potential calendar salesman.

Warren Lincoln had been found.

He was living in a nice apartment near Lake Michigan. Lincoln's cheeks had hollowed out, and his shoulders drooped. Detective A.J. Wirz and Kane County Assistant State Attorney J. Bruce Amell brought Lincoln to the police station and started some preliminary questioning.

When police asked about the last time he saw his wife's brother, Byron, Lincoln squirmed a bit.

"He isn't living," Lincoln said flatly. "Well boys, I want to make a clean breast of it, and tell you the whole thing. It has been worrying me for a long time. I'll begin at the beginning. The night this happened, I noticed I was the only one served cocoa."

Lincoln said he was suspicious and refused to drink the hot chocolate. Byron flew into a rage, but Lina suddenly appeared. She shot her brother three times. Lincoln grabbed the gun and then hit her on the head with a fire poker.

He was afraid. Not knowing what to do, Lincoln decided to cut up both bodies and burn them in his furnace. Finally, he spread chicken blood on the window sill and faked his death to escape from the entire horrible episode.

Lincoln's words came out breathlessly. The newspaper reported it was as if a spigot had been pulled from a barrel unexpectedly. It was a vibrant, shocking story from beginning to end.

Two thousand miles away in San Francisco, Michels picked up a local paper. The case he had worked on for months had apparently been solved. A telegram from the Aurora police saying Lincoln had confessed followed. But Michels found Lincoln's story a little *too* perfect. In it, Lincoln was a victim and the evidence was burned. There was literally no *corpus dilecti* (body of evidence).

A jailer serves tea to Aurora Police Chief Frank Michels (left) and Warren Lincoln (center, seated). Beacon-News *archives.*

Michels's gut wasn't satisfied as he headed back to Aurora. Warren Lincoln's confession changed little at first. Lincoln said he burned the bodies in his furnace and scattered the ashes on his driveway.

But the next day, Lincoln said, after having given it some thought, that he may have put the ashes in the city dump.

Day after day after day, Michels sat in the cell with Lincoln, who was being held on a theft charge. Michels put his hand on Lincoln's shoulder and listened, gently pointing out anything that didn't make sense.

"I have told the truth," Lincoln said, sobbing. "I can't help it if you don't believe."

Outside the police department, the public eyed Michels suspiciously. Michels was trying to outwit Lincoln, a former lawyer, a man who evaded police for months, a man with a vivid imagination. Maybe the chief was no match. Inside headquarters, officers suggested Michels had gone soft. Was this really the same chief who yelled at the mayor when he tried to cut officers' pay? Now he was treating a killer like a friend. Put a little muscle to him, officers said to each other, and then Lincoln would tell the truth.

For two weeks, Lincoln and Michels sat in a tiny cell as Lincoln told lie after lie. Maybe both Lina and Byron were alive. Or it was Byron who killed Lina.

"You know, Warren," Michels said, after thirteen days and five confessions, "I don't believe a word of it. I am going to do the best I can for you as a friend. The truth will come out. For the sake of your own peace of mind, tell it to me."

"Oh all right, you've been a good fellow," Lincoln finally said. "I'll tell you the truth."

In detail, Lincoln calmly told his secret to his only friend in the world.

"Yes, but Warren, you've told so many stories," Michels replied. "How do I know this one is true? I want facts. Show me."

THE TRIP TO THE DUMP

On January 26, 1924, Lincoln, Michels and a gaggle of photographers headed for the city dump on Lake Street. Wearing a winter hat, the chief walked through the garbage, while Lincoln smoked a cigarette and pointed. You're warm, he assured the chief. A little to the north.

Finally, police found two wooden crates, both about two feet long and weighing about 150 pounds each. Inside the crates were two cement blocks. Lincoln fainted.

City officials carried the blocks out of the dump and hauled them half a mile back to city hall. Jacob Johansen was brought in from the water department to break them open. The sledgehammer pounded on the first block until the block split down the middle, revealing Lincoln's secret.

A terrible smell filled the room. People gasped and shuddered.

Johansen took a huge swing at the second block.

WHACK.

As Johansen worked, Lincoln's secret spread on the street.

WHACK.

Hundreds of people headed to city hall to see for themselves.

WHACK.

It was almost too horrifying to believe on word-of-mouth alone. It had to be seen.

WHACK.

The second wooden crate opened with a crack. The men who had stood their ground while the first block was opened backed away. The smell was pungent, repulsive even, but the sight was worse.

The block had split in half. One half crumbled to the ground, bits of hair still caught in the stone. In the other half, spectators saw the well-preserved heads of Lina Lincoln and Byron Shoup.

THE UNLIKELY WITNESS

Ray Demmitt hadn't spent much time in the spotlight.

During a lackluster seventh place season in 1914, the University of Illinois graduate patrolled left field for the White Sox. Then, nine games into his next season, he was gone, with hardly a mention in the press.

But on January 27, 1924, Demmitt was surrounded by reporters. That day, he had the unpleasant task of identifying two relatives—Lina Lincoln and Byron Shoup, his wife's aunt and uncle—by looking at their decapitated heads.

Lina's husband admitted to shooting them both, cutting up the bodies and encasing their heads in cement and dropping the blocks in the city dump.

"One glance was all I needed," Demmitt said. "I am positive that they are the heads of Aunt Lina and Uncle Byron, as my wife called them. Oh, what a sight!"

Lincoln, who fainted when the heads were found, had returned to good spirits, eating lunch with Michels and posing for pictures for the newspaper.

White Sox outfield Ray Demmitt. *Library of Congress.*

Warren told Michels he used the cement blocks to prop up his porch for months, until guilt motivated him to remove the evidence. It was another strange story.

"He has been telling first one wild yarn and then another to lay the foundation for an insanity defense," said Kane County Assistant State Attorney J. Bruce Amell. "He has perfect comprehension of right and wrong. As a fact, the unusual action was dictated by the cunning of a crafty slayer."

Like any previously unimaginable tragedy, the public was horrified and captivated. How could someone commit a deed so gruesome? And, more importantly, why? Reporters rushed to Michels, who had spent weeks with Lincoln, slowly coaxing a confession out of him. Surely he had a sense of Lincoln's sanity. But the chief begged off.

"Men much more schooled in medicine than I will have to pass on this man," Michels said. "He may be a Dr. Jekyll and Mr. Hyde, in some moments timid and weak, and in others a man of tremendous cruelty and power and cunning. That he is of a most unusual type, all the world can tell."

At the October 1924 sanity hearing, Lincoln's lawyer said his client was "crazier than hell."

But the state portrayed Lincoln as a crafty killer. He is, Kane County State Attorney Charles Abbott said, "the prince of prevaricators." It's not recorded whether the jury knew Abbott was just calling Lincoln a big liar, but they got the point. After less than two hours of deliberation, they declared Lincoln fit to stand trial.

Now jurors were forced to answer the questions that confound anyone who looks at an act of evil. If so much planning had gone into the murders (covering up the crime, evading police), didn't that suggest a devious and rational mind? But how could an act so repulsive be the work of a sane person? If Lincoln was sane, are we all capable of such unspeakable acts?

The debate was more than a philosophical one. If he was insane, Lincoln would spend his life in prison. If declared sane, he would be put to death.

The trial was courtroom drama at its most frenzied. The gruesome murders, Lincoln's wild lies and Lincoln's tenuous connection to the sixteenth president of the United States brought out rubberneckers, speculators, onlookers and snoopers. The case was so notorious and the legal issues so complex it took 8 days and 375 tries before 12 men could be found who professed to be unbiased enough to sit on the jury.

Warren Lincoln (second from left) sits with his legal team. Beacon-News *archives.*

Crowds stood in the hallways of the Geneva courthouse just to listen to the opening statements echo through the open doors. Seventy-five extra chairs were brought in for "trial fans," older women and high school girls who brought a lunch with them rather than give up a good seat during the break.

And the lawyers, particularly Charles Abbott, rose to the occasion, using verbiage he had apparently been saving for just the right case. Abbott told the jury Lincoln was a "rank liar" and a "cunning, crafty weaver of lies," who should be "stamped out as any pestilence."

"How are you going to face the people of this county unless you bring in a verdict that will hang this man by the neck until he is dead, dead, dead!" Abbott implored.

Aurora's mayor, doctors, detectives, the city jailer, handwriting experts, medical doctors and psychiatrists all testified for prosecutors. Even a minister's wife took the stand and said Warren was sane and responsible for his crimes and should be executed. Even Lincoln testified, telling a shocked courtroom that he, in fact, hadn't killed anyone at all. Lincoln's lawyers admitted their client's guilt but begged the jury to vote against hanging. Surely they could see Lincoln was a lunatic? Send him to prison, yes, but spare his life.

The jury must have been spinning trying to sort out whether this man should be put to death for a devil's plan or sympathetically removed from society and sent to prison for life. They needed someone calm and rational to explain a monster.

The witness the defense found was, at first blush, the most unlikely.

To convince the jury, the defense depended on a man who had spent months peering into the killer's psyche. For the first time in his long career, Frank Michels was called to testify for the defense. That infuriated the prosecutor.

"Did it ever occur to you, chief, that Lincoln thought you had a soft spot in your head and was trying to deceive you?" Abbott asked.

"In *your* head," Michels answered hotly, with the emphasis on the second word.

"Now don't get angry," Abbott replied, still on the attack. "I didn't say you had a soft spot in your head. I said: Did the thought occur to you that Lincoln might have thought so?"

"Oh, that's it," Michels said. "If I misunderstood, I apologize. Anyways, that's a foolish question to ask anybody."

Abbott continued pushing the chief. He made Michels walk the jury through Lincoln's many lies, his elaborate efforts to cover his tracks after he killed and cut up his wife and brother-in-law. But Michels insisted Lincoln was crazy.

"You have an interest in this case, have you not?" Abbott asked.

"I have a conscience, that's all," Michels answered flatly.

The jury studied Michels, a man who staked his legacy of four decades of brilliant police work on this one bizarre case. He had spent years tracking evidence and then weeks coaxing a confession out of Lincoln. And in the end, Michels asked for compassion, not vengeance. Two deaths were enough. Executing Lincoln would not bring them back.

Warren Lincoln (left) and Aurora police chief Frank Michels. Beacon-News *archives*.

After five ballots and more than three hours of deliberation, the jury returned.

"We, the jury, find Warren J. Lincoln, guilty of murder," clerk Charles Farmiloe announced. He paused before reading the sentence. "Imprisonment for the rest of his natural life."

Out of madness, the jury had found mercy.

THE END OF A CAREER

Lincoln spent the rest of his life in prison. Although he first told reporters he was angry about the verdict and furious with Michels for calling him insane, Lincoln quickly gave up an appeal.

On February 9, 1925, he became prisoner No. 9632 at Joliet State Penitentiary. The prison's warden quickly found a suitable assignment for the man famous for his gladiolus and sweet peas.

"Lincoln has been assigned to the general duties in the prison yard," the warden's secretary announced. "There are flower beds to be taken care of."

After sixteen years in prison, Lincoln failed to recover from gallbladder surgery and died in prison. He was sixty-two. Three years after he took the stand in defense of Lincoln and shortly after a second Aurora officer was killed on the city's streets, Michels announced his retirement.

By April 1928, Michels had served a remarkable forty years in the department, most of which as chief of police. The *Beacon-News* estimated he had worked on 100,000 cases. The city's booster club planned a huge celebration where they presented Michels with a two-carat diamond ring and $1,500 in gold—more than a year's pension.

Police chiefs from across Illinois came to the ceremony held at the Fox Theater. At the end of the event, Michels addressed the crowd. He looked back on a career that started in a farming town and ended in a city, with all the good and bad that entails.

"I do not know that I am deserving of such marks, but I am very grateful," he said. "I only have done what I thought was my duty, and my one aim throughout my life has been to do as nearly right as my conscience told me. I am glad to say, after forty years [in] the department, that I have never been guilty of a dishonest act, or a taken a dishonest dollar."

"When I entered the service, Aurora was little more than a village," he said. "It did not have the police problems that it has today...Facilities were not so good, in those days, for a criminal to make a getaway. If he wanted to get out of town he either had to go on the Burlington or walk. There were not the hard roads and the fast automobiles of today, giving opportunity [for] a fugitive to run to Chicago in an hour and bury himself in that great city."

After the ceremony, Michels was made honorary detective and given the power to act in that capacity any time he pleased. He told the newspaper he had earned a rest and planned a motor trip through the South and West with his wife and son.

Unfortunately, his life without a badge didn't last long.

Michels died nineteen months later, in his home on Lake Street at the age of sixty-four. Solving the Lincoln murders was mentioned in the obituaries that ran in dozens of Illinois newspapers. The story was retold—not to remember a madman but to illustrate Michels's courage and diligence, honesty and kindness.

"His word was good as his bond," stated a *Beacon* editorial published on the day Michels died. "He never went back on a friend. He saved grownups and young from themselves. The epitaph might well be his: He loved and served."

The Two Burials of Three-Fingered Hamilton

The second time they buried Three-Fingered Red Hamilton, it was a solemn event and there was a priest.

They held the second funeral early on a Saturday morning, hoping to avoid the press and the people who hated Hamilton so much they wouldn't have dropped a grudge just because he was dead.

John Klein, the pastor at Oswego Presbyterian Church, agreed to perform the service.

Besides Father Klein, three policemen were in attendance, along with the grave digger, the grave digger's assistant, a *Beacon-News* reporter and a woman who said she was Hamilton's mother but turned out to be a crazy lady who stalked gangsters' funerals.

They gathered at a secluded section of the cemetery, a peaceful hollow surrounded by trees. The casket was covered in a gray cloth.

"We consign this body to the grave and to the dust from whence it came," Klein said.

All in all, this second funeral was an improvement on Hamilton's first burial. Attendance was up, and it was in a real cemetery, as opposed to a gravel pit. The benediction was even more powerful, if less personal, than what John Dillinger had muttered while pouring lye on his friend's dead body sixteen months earlier.

One funeral is predictable. Two funerals is, at the very least, unexpected. And Red Hamilton's was a particularly improbable long shot because his friends had gone out of their way to make the first one stick.

But then a doctor was held for ransom, a gambler hit a cop in the face with a mug of beer and, well, that's how these things happen.

THE SECRET GRAVE

John Dillinger. *FBI archives.*

In attendance at the first funeral of Three-Fingered Red Hamilton, held in April 1934, were:

John Dillinger: bank robber; murderer of cops, prison guards and innocent bystanders; Public Enemy No. 1.

Doc Barker: thief; robber; murderer; kidnapper; future Alcatraz prisoner.

Homer van Meter: bank robber.

William Weaver: paroled cop killer; kidnapper; bank robber.

Harry Campbell: bank robber.

Volney Davis: gambler, bank robber.

So Hamilton was among friends. They had come together on this sort-of solemn occasion to honor and desecrate the body of Hamilton, age thirty-four at his time of death, a man who had distinguished himself as a proficient bank robber and ruthless killer. For those who had seen Hamilton and lived, they could hardly forget his flat face, his pug nose or the two fingers that were missing on his right hand due to a childhood sledding incident.

John "Red" Hamilton was born in Canada and eventually made his way to Indiana, where he was imprisoned for robbing a gas station and where he would meet Dillinger, who was sentenced to ten years for robbing a grocery store.

Apparently, neither man particularly liked jail. They managed to free each other in separate, daring raids. With Dillinger as the public face and Hamilton as his preferred gunman, the gang began robbing banks across the Midwest and generally embarrassing the Federal Bureau of Investigation. Between the summer of 1933 and April 1934, Dillinger and Hamilton robbed banks in Bluffton and New Carlisle, Ohio; Greencastle, Indianapolis, Dalesville and Montpelier, Indiana; Racine, Wisconsin; East Chicago, Indiana (where they killed a police officer and Hamilton was shot); Sioux Falls, South Dakota; and Mason City, Iowa (where Hamilton was shot again).

By April 1934, the feds had finally built an operation coordinated enough to identify and track these robbers. J. Edgar Hoover assigned his best man, Melvin Purvis, to track down Dillinger's gang. Purvis zeroed in on them at the Little Bohemia Lodge in far northern Wisconsin. The raid would turn out to be one of the federal government's most public debacles. A civilian and a federal agent were killed, while Dillinger, Hamilton and Baby Face Nelson escaped.

Dillinger and Hamilton were unharmed, but they were now hunted. They stuck to back roads in Wisconsin and Minnesota, stealing cars as needed. On Monday, April 23, about twenty miles south of St. Paul, Minnesota, a policeman spotted Dillinger's car. The officer gave chase at 80 miles per hour, trading shots with the criminals. Hamilton was hit in the back. The bullet pierced his spinal column but didn't kill him.

With Hamilton bleeding in the back seat, Dillinger had to flee. They headed for Illinois.

THE AURORA CONNECTION

Volney Davis went by many names: Curly Davis, Cotton Davis, E.V. Davis, Everett Davis, J.H. Lockwood, S.S. Lockwood, C.E. Moore, Jimmy Curley Moore, J.E. Hansen and Roy Green. But while he was living in his Aurora apartment at 415 Fox Street, everybody called him Curley Hansen.

And everybody—particularly gamblers and tavern owners—knew Curley Hansen. He had blond hair, blue eyes, a long face and a prominent jaw line. When he showed up at a bar, he bought drinks for the house and tipped waitresses $20.

At seventeen years old, Davis had been sentenced to life in prison for a robbery in which a night watchman had been killed. He served nine years before applying for an eight-month jail leave and then a one-year extension, and then he decided not to return at all.

By that time, Davis had met up with members of the Barker-Karpis gang, an enterprising group who had found kidnapping wealthy people and holding them for ransom to be lucrative business.

In January 1934, Davis helped kidnap a Minnesota doctor. The kidnappers held the doctor for $200,000 ransom, which was paid shortly before John Dillinger showed up at Davis's Aurora apartment with a dying Hamilton. Dillinger and Hamilton, looking for a hideout, had been turned down by two members of the Capone syndicate, who suggested Davis to be a suitable alternative. And so it was in Davis's apartment near Fox and Fourth Streets—

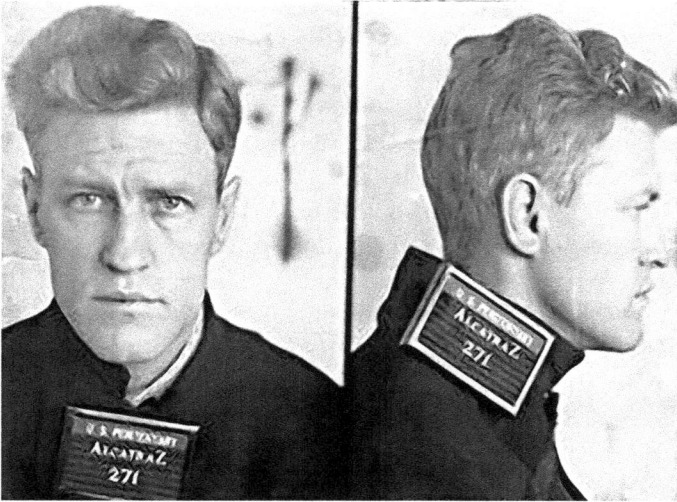

Volney Davis.
*Courtesy of the
Alcatraz Alumni
Association.*

ten days after he had been shot—that Hamilton's crime career permanently ended at 3:00 p.m. on April 30, 1934.

At sundown, Davis went to a small gravel pit in a desolate area near Oswego and spent about forty-five minutes helping dig a grave. Around 9:00 p.m., six heavily armed men drove a dead body that was dressed in a blue twill suit, a coat and low-cut black leather shoes to the gravel pit.

Standing over Hamilton's body, in a low voice, Dillinger said, "Red, old pal, I hate to do this, but I know you'd do the same for me." Dillinger then started pouring cans of lye on Hamilton's face and hands so no one would ever recognize him.

The area was leveled off and Davis placed a roll of barbed wire on the spot as the only marker. Over the years, grass grew up around the undiscovered grave. Even among other thieves, Dillinger would say Hamilton was buried in the dunes of Lake Michigan.

And Hamilton might still be in that gravel pit, if a plane hadn't made an emergency landing in Yorkville.

THE UNEXPECTED LANDING

The federal government tends to have a good memory for things like kidnapping well-known doctors and holding them for ransom. And so, in February 1935, agents from the Bureau of Investigation captured former

Aurora resident Volney Davis in Kansas City, Missouri, and decided to fly him back to Minnesota to face conspiracy charges.

What followed was a most amazing convergence of bad luck and sheer incompetence. While flying north from Missouri to Minnesota, darkness and haze forced the pilot to make an emergency landing in a Yorkville farm field. In a flight that was supposed to cover 450 miles, the pilot had landed within walking distance of Davis's old Aurora apartment.

What was going through the agents' minds is unclear, but they were clearly nervous about their unexpected landing. They ordered the driver who picked them up in the field to turn off his lights and keep his mouth shut. They refused to take Davis to the Kendall County Jail, instead ordering the driver to head for the nearest public phone so they could call in for instructions.

They ended up at the Nading Hotel Bar in Yorkville where, inexplicably, they removed Davis's handcuffs. One of the agents headed for the phone booth while Davis convinced the other agent to buy him a beer. Two beers were drawn and the agent raised his stein.

"Here's to you," the agent said.

"And here's to you," Davis replied and then smashed the agent in the face with his mug before jumping through a plate glass window and fleeing into the snowy streets he knew well.

It would be more than three months before the feds found Davis in Chicago. Davis quickly pled guilty to the kidnapping. He was alone and facing a long sentence when he wrote home.

"It has been awful to be running around all over the country and not being able to write to the only ones in this world that really love me...I will be sentenced this week, I don't know what I will get but I expect it will be a life sentence."

Davis once again had long odds on getting out of prison. Within two months of pleading guilty, he was ready to offer the feds the key to a mystery that had taunted them for years: He knew where the last of Dillinger's pals was buried.

The Grave Diggers

By August 1935, John Dillinger and Baby Face Nelson had been killed by policemen. The rest of the Dillinger gang were dead or in prison. But no one seemed to know what had happened to Three-Fingered Red Hamilton.

Rumors swirled that he had been buried in Galena, Illinois, or Missouri or thrown in a Wisconsin lime kiln. Some said he was still alive but paralyzed.

For three days, hardly anyone noticed the four men poking around in a gravel pit close to where the Burlington Railroad passed over Route 25 near Oswego.

Following a rough map drawn by Volney Davis, the agents found the secret grave of Hamilton on August 28, 1935. Grass and weeds had grown over the area. After digging in different spots, an agent uncovered an arm bone (missing parts of two fingers) about two feet underground.

Agents excavated the body, some blue twill fabric, a can of lye and a horseshoe. They identified the body as Hamilton's using dental records. The last of Dillinger's men was officially dead.

Sonny Boy's Blues

Since it opened in 1928, the Leland Hotel has been the centerpiece of Aurora's skyline. For decades, it was the tallest building in the state outside of Chicago. When it was built, the cost of furnishing the 200 rooms totaled $100,000; the linens cost another $100,000.

The crown on this suburban skyscraper was the ballroom on the nineteenth floor. In there, the walls were red, green and black. The ceiling was painted like the night sky, with each wrought-iron light fixture representing a different star or planet. Through the tall arched windows, visitors could see to the end of the horizon. The buzzing world below looked peaceful from two hundred feet up.

But on May 5, 1937—the most important day in the Leland's history—the view was dull and uninspiring. It had rained for weeks. It had poured for so long that pastors held special sessions asking God to give it a rest. The foul weather didn't matter much to the three musicians who had set up a temporary recording studio in the empty ballroom. They weren't from Aurora, and they weren't making a record for people in Aurora. In fact, most of the city had never heard of these three men.

If Aurorans had understood what was happening, they would have stood in the pouring rain just to get a glimpse of Sonny Boy Williamson, Robert Nighthawk and Big Joe Williams leaving the Leland. They would have bribed a doorman to let them sit in the stairwell and listen to these men lay down sixteen tracks in less than four hours.

There, above the city, history was being made. An eavesdropper wouldn't have even had to wait very long to hear a masterpiece. It was the very first song recorded.

John Lee "Sonny Boy" Williamson, a twenty-three-year-old harmonica player who liked to gamble and drink, started the session, with Nighthawk and Williams on guitar behind him.

Williamson was brilliant on the harmonica, an instrument he'd been playing since he was a child in Tennessee. Before May 5, 1937, the harmonica was background, a nice accent on blues music's dirty vocals. It was a novelty instrument that hung around with kazoos, jugs and washboards. That day, the harmonica moved from its role as a supporting instrument to the lead role.

Around 11:00 a.m., Williamson played the first notes of his song, "Good Morning, School Girl." Behind him, a guitar provided a steady bum-dum-de-dum. Williamson, who was known to stomp so hard while playing he would put pillows under his feet to muffle the sound, let his harmonica dance for twenty-seven seconds. Then, in his deep Southern drawl, Williamson answered:

> *Hello little school girl,*
> *Good morning little school girl,*
> *Can I go home with you?*
> *Can I go home with you?*
> *Now you can tell your mother and your father, mmm,*
> *that Sonny Boy's a little school boy, too*

Seventy-five years later, artists are still recording versions of that three-minute song. Buddy Guy, Junior Wells, the Grateful Dead, Muddy Waters, Van Morrison and Rod Stewart have put it on their albums. The song has been inducted into the Blues Hall of Fame, along with all three men who played on it.

And yet, on May 5, 1937, the three musicians passed through Aurora unnoticed. While "Good Morning, School Girl" set off a firestorm in black America, its birthplace was obscured and the song's author was overshadowed. It took monumental efforts to revive the legend of Sonny Boy Williamson. By then, being murdered wasn't even the worst thing that had happened to him.

"ALL RIGHT, JOHN"

Exactly how and why Sonny Boy Williamson ended up sitting in the ballroom of the Leland Hotel is a bit of a mystery. Williamson, Nighthawk and Big Joe had been hired by producer Lester Melrose, a controversial figure who managed to record some great early blues artists while claiming their composition copyrights. Melrose handled most of RCA Records Bluebird label artists and ran a tight ship. At the May 5 Leland session, each man recorded at least four songs and then rotated to play on another man's record.

In 1937, RCA didn't have a studio in Chicago, so it wasn't uncommon to use hotels for recordings. Drop in a few chairs and a couple microphones, and you were ready to go. In fact, the day before Williamson's memorable set, Tampa Red and Washboard Sam had recorded sixteen songs in one Leland session. These men were part of the first ripples in a tidal wave of black musicians headed to Chicago.

Williamson had grown up on a farm in Madison County, Tennessee. At age eleven, he received a harmonica from his mother for Christmas. At the time, amateur musicians were buying millions of harmonicas in the United States each year. The appeal was obvious: harmonicas were cheap (about ten cents in 1925), relatively easy to learn and even easier to carry.

As a boy, when Williamson wasn't doing his chores, he was playing along with his records. At school, he would gather classmates under an oak tree to make music during recess, dust flying from up from their feet as they stomped out beats.

By age sixteen, he was jamming with prominent blues musicians like Yank Rachell and Sleepy John Estes. He traveled to St. Louis, Memphis and New Orleans. And he began to stretch the harmonica's muscle. He started playing crossed-harp, using the draw notes (the ones played while breathing in) to widen the range of playable sounds. By 1934, Williamson was a skilled harmonica player who could write and sing. And although he had grown up poor in the Jim Crow South, Williamson's songs don't seem to carry the same worldly pain as other blues musicians. His early songs are joyous celebrations of sexual yearning and drunkenness. In several, Williamson yells out "All right, John!" before breaking into a harmonica solo, as if his harmonica self and singing self are in competition.

Williamson liked to drink and loved to gamble, but it didn't seem to hurt his career. He was reliable enough that he attracted the attention of Melrose, who asked him to record at the Leland. That session, which also included blues standards like "Sugar Mama" and "Blue Bird Blues," made him an icon. When Muddy Waters came to Chicago, his first gig was with Sonny Boy Williamson. And in Louisiana, a young musician named Marion Jacobs—who later, as Little Walter, would revolutionize blues harmonica by playing into an amplifier—tried to imitate the Sonny Boy sound.

"COME ON UP"

In Chicago in the late 1930s, the majority of the African-American population lived in a five- to six-block strip that ran from Wentworth Avenue to Lake Michigan. If you wanted to hear or buy black music, you went there.

The biggest and best shop was Rols, a huge building that covered a city block. When William Arnold got a little money, he'd head straight for the store's RCA section and flip past the green labels (oriental music) and red labels (classical) until he hit a real prize: the blue label of Bluebird's race records. For forty cents, Arnold could take home music performed by people who looked like him and understood his life.

That's probably how Williamson first ended up in Arnold's collection. Right away, Arnold was drawn in by the unusual, rough voice. It sounded like he was singing right to Arnold. He wore that record out and Williamson's next few, too.

So you can imagine what a thrill it was when, at twelve years old, Arnold learned that some family members knew his hero. Arnold's father said Williamson had recently played at a relative's club and tore the place up; people threw money at him when he took the stage. Not only that, but Williamson lived nearby.

The proximity was too much for Arnold ignore. He talked to a guitar player who knew where Williamson lived. One afternoon, after seeing a movie, Arnold convinced his two friends to knock on the door at 3226 South Giles Avenue. A tall, strong man answered the door.

"We're looking for Sonny Boy Williamson," Arnold said.

"This is Sonny Boy Williamson."

"We want to hear you play harmonica."

"Well, come on up."

For more than hour, Williamson showed the boys the basics of blues harmonica and took requests from their favorite records.

"Did that sound like me?" Williamson joked after each song.

Williamson invited the boys to watch him perform sometime. When Arnold showed up a few weeks later, Williamson invited the boy in like they were old friends.

A few more weeks passed, and Arnold decided to return for a third lesson. When he arrived, Arnold asked the landlady if Sonny Boy was home.

"Hadn't you heard?" she said. "He got killed."

"LORD HAVE MERCY"

At 2:30 a.m. on June 1, 1948, the doorbell rang at 3226 South Giles Avenue. Lacey Belle Williamson opened the door and found her husband leaning against the wall, holding his head. His hat was missing and his clothes were dirty, as if he had been rolling on the ground. He was bleeding from the mouth and had a bruise over his left eye.

She asked what happened. Williamson went inside and sat on the bed.

"Lord have mercy," was all he would say.

Investigators later determined Williamson had been playing a raucous set at the nearby Plantation Club. At 2:00 a.m., the owner finally stopped him by pulling him off stage. Williamson stuck the microphone in his pocket and said he was heading home. The police record picks up again when he rang his doorbell.

While Williamson sat on the bed, Lacey Belle started washing the blood off and again asked what had happened.

"I'm dying," he said but offered no other details. At 5:00 a.m., he lost consciousness. He was dead before he ever got to the hospital.

When detectives first examined the body, his injuries—a bruise over his eye and a scrape on his head—seemed so insignificant they weren't sure they had a murder. It wasn't until the autopsy that the coroner was able to determine Williamson had died "as the result of fractures of the skull and intra-cranial hemorrhag[ing]...caused when the deceased was brutally assaulted."

Most likely, Williamson was jumped on his way home. His wallet, a yellow gold Bulova watch, a ring, three harmonicas and the microphone were missing. Two men were arrested. They passed lie detector tests. No one was ever charged.

Williamson's death became a legend that obscured the facts. Blues musician Lonnie Johnson heard Williamson ended up with seventeen holes in his head from an ice pick. Another story that floated around held Williamson was jumped for the three pearl-inlay harmonicas he always carried. Another was that he hit on a woman whose boyfriend took exception. Maybe he won more than $1,000 gambling, and some other jealous musicians jumped him.

"Most of the musicians were jealous. They didn't have his talent, his stage presence," said Arnold, who, at seventy-six years old, is now a prominent blues harmonica player. "He had more talent than Howlin' Wolf, Muddy Waters—all those guys."

At this point, the why and how of Williamson's death are likely unknowable. Only the what-ifs remain. Williamson was just beginning to experiment with electric amplification, the next evolution in blues music.

"There's just so much missed possibilities because of his death," said Michael Baker, a librarian who helped start the Shannon Street Blues Festival in Williamson's home town. "He was just way ahead of his time. If you listen to his music chronologically, you see such growth. I don't think there was a whole lot of people—especially in the white community—that knew Sonny Boy. And the Rice Miller thing really messed things up."

It wasn't bad enough somebody took Sonny Boy's life. Somebody had to take his name, too.

"The One and Only"

The great irony of Rice Miller is that he could really play. In the 1930s, billed as "Boy Blue," he shone alongside great blues musicians, including Robert Johnson. Miller was so good he could put the skinny end of the harmonica in his mouth and play with no hands. It's undisputed that any list of the greatest blues harmonica players must include Rice Miller. But you'll probably never see his name on such a list. Instead, you'll see Sonny Boy Williamson II. It's unimaginable today but, just before he became famous, Rice Miller borrowed the name of the best-known blues harmonica player and then never gave it back.

The exact reasons for the deception aren't clear, but it's probably not hard to guess. In 1941, Miller was a brilliant musician without a record who was offered a spot on a local Arkansas radio show.

"John Lee (Williamson) has records on the juke box. If you want to sell tickets, then you're Sonny Boy," Baker said.

Billed as Sonny Boy Williamson, Miller was the star of the King Biscuit Hour, a hugely influential blues radio show. In black sections of the South, so many homes tuned in, it was said you could walk for miles and never miss a note.

Perhaps Miller's deception started innocently. Bill Donaghue, who wrote a book on Rice Miller, suggests friends started calling him Sonny Boy as a tribute.

"If you played guitar and acted like Elvis Presley, your friends would call you Elvis Presley," he said.

No matter the reason, in 1941, the world was big enough for two Sonny Boys. A Sonny Boy Williamson could be a famous blues harmonica player in Chicago, and another Sonny Boy Williamson could be famous in Arkansas without much interference.

Sonny Boy's Blues

There's solid anecdotal evidence the two men knew each other and, in some way, Sonny Boy Williamson allowed Rice Miller to use the name. Williamson's brother told Baker that the original Williamson just didn't really care. And by the time he was killed, it was too late for Miller; he had made his name with someone else's name, so the deception accelerated. Miller began calling himself "the one and only Sonny Boy Williamson,"—a misleading but by then accurate statement—and moved his birth date back to make himself older. As the years went on, Williamson's friends bristled.

After a show in 1951, Arnold confronted Miller about using the name. Arnold said Miller panicked and started saying Arnold was trying to steal his job.

"All he had to say was I admired the man's music and using his name afforded me to make a living," Arnold said. "He really made a fool of himself."

In the 1960s, when British acts like the Rolling Stones started recording old blues tunes, forgotten Chicago musicians were suddenly in demand. Miller became a worldwide star, playing alongside the Yardbirds in front of huge audiences. The two Sonny Boy stories (and possibly their recording rights) began to mingle. The real Sonny Boy was fading away.

When Williamson died, he was just another wild, black musician who got himself killed. The *Chicago Tribune* made no mention of his murder. His body was shipped back to Jackson, where four sentences in the classified section announced funeral plans under the headline "Colored dead." Williamson was buried at the end of a gravel road under a huge tree. A simple metal post with a handwritten note was the only marker.

Over the years, deep green kudzu crept over the cemetery, and Rice Miller's fame crept over Williamson's name, until he was almost lost. But in the late 1980s, a young librarian reading about the history of rock 'n' roll was stopped in his tracks by a brief mention that the great Sonny Boy Williamson was buried in Madison County, Tennessee. How come I've never seen his grave? Michael Baker wondered. He began to poke around and found that Williamson's half-brother, T.W. Utley, was still living in town. A few weeks later, Utley was driving Baker to the rusty forty-year-old metal grave marker.

"This man did so much for music, and his hometown doesn't know who he is," Baker remembers thinking as he drove away. "This guy deserves better."

The Madison County library staff started a fundraising campaign to buy a headstone. On a whim, Baker called RCA to see if the company would contribute. He ended up speaking with Billy Altman, a blues aficionado who was searching RCA's vaults for Williamson's songs, in anticipation of releasing a compilation. Within days, Altman had approached a vice-president at RCA who simply suggested they order a headstone and let him know how much it cost.

"It's one of the things I'm probably most proud of in my career," said Altman, who now teaches in the humanities department at the School of Visual Arts in New York. "I kind of shamed a pretty big record company into giving a little drop in the bucket."

"ROMEO AND JULIET"

On June 1, 1990, Baker, Altman and about two dozen family members and friends held the first Sonny Boy Williamson Day in Tennessee. A historical marker was placed alongside Highway 18, and harmonicas were laid at Williamson's new headstone. And, of course, Williamson's biggest hit was performed.

In the seventy-five years since "Good Morning, School Girl" was recorded in Aurora, the song has been covered hundreds of times. Even as memories of Williamson faded, his song's stature grew. How did a three-minute song recorded in an empty ballroom become a blues standard?

"It's a universal theme: Guy likes girl. Girl might like guy, might not. Girl's family definitely does not like guy," said Baker. "That's Romeo and Juliet with a blues harmonica."

And in most versions recorded since 1937, the singer plays up a salacious older man promising a diamond ring and a trip around the world to a little schoolgirl. In that interpretation, some of the lightness in the original is lost. Like most of Williamson's songs, "Good Morning" was personal; he was singing about a real heartbreak.

In 1946, music historian Alan Lomax recorded a conversation between Williamson, Big Bill Broonzy and Memphis Slim. The men talked candidly about growing up in the South and blues music. At one point, Broonzy asks Williamson why he started singing the blues.

"Well, I tell you, Bill," Williamson responds, "I used to have a sweet little girl, you know, her name [was] Estelle. We used to go to school together... Grew up together, in other words. I wanted to love her and ask her mother for her and, why, she turned me down and that caused me to sing the blues. See, I couldn't get her. See, so I thought of a little school girl because me and this girl used to go to school together, you know? Her parents thought I wasn't the right boy for her, you understand, and wouldn't make her happy and everything. So they turned me down. And just got to sitting down and thinking, you understand? And then I thought of a song and I started drinking. And then I started to sing it."

Revisionist history? Maybe. But it's a mistake to dismiss "Good Morning" as a simple teenage love song, especially since the story is hung on a surprisingly complicated structure.

Nearly all blues music is 8-, 12-, or 16-bar blues. It's a sound that hits the ear naturally. But Williamson did something a bit different in "Good Morning, School Girl." As he hit the last two words of "Can I go home *with you?*" he takes a song that seemed headed for a standard 12-bar composition and instead drops back two beats into a swift, sweet riff.

Adam Gussow, a blues musician and professor at the University of Mississippi who has given performance lectures on Sonny Boy's music, says it's a unique creature: a 9-½ bar blues song.

"It makes the listener think it's one kind of blues and it switches," he said. "It feels organic, but it's unique."

Blues historians often refer to Williamson as simple, likely because of his slow, almost slurred speaking style, his easygoing manner and reckless lifestyle. But you have to look no further than his first song, with its elusive (and therefore alluring) structure. The song sticks because it gives you an unexpected lead instrument in unconventional arrangement. That's why so many keep returning to it. That's how it became part of the blues DNA.

"If you're playing off Little Walter licks, then you're indirectly playing off John Lee Sonny Boy Williamson because Little Walter learned from him," Arnold said. "Before 'Good Morning, School Girl,' nobody played the harmonica with any popularity on records. 'Good Morning, School Girl' brought another voice to the blues."

On a rainy day in Aurora, Sonny Boy Williamson made sure the harmonica would never be just a child's toy.

"I don't think you could do that with a kazoo. I don't think I want to hear that," Baker said. "Pretty much anyone who does blues on the (harmonica) owes a debt to Sonny Boy."

Leap Year Ladies

It's a little known fact that Aurora was one of the first Illinois cities to have a woman serve as mayor. In truth, Aurora has had at least thirteen female mayors—each serving a one-day term as part of a tradition that, today, might seem offensive, politically incorrect and completely foreign to anyone born after the "powder puff council" ruled.

But back in 1940, when Audre' Kesel sat behind the mayor's desk, things weren't so sophisticated.

"It was a smaller town and people knew each other," she said. "And it was a heck of a lot of fun."

From 1932 to 1980, with a break for World War II, Aurora celebrated Leap Day by putting bachelorettes on the city council and women in the police and fire departments for a single day. Along the way, hundreds of bachelors were "arrested," thousands of dollars were raised and Aurora drew the nation's attention.

In 2008, from her home in Sugar Grove, the eighty-eight year old reminisced about her big day.

She recalled there was one good-looking bachelor who was "arrested" and couldn't be released until he brought bail from the Lietz & Grometer general store.

"I sent him over to get some nylons," she said. "Not one pair—I wanted three!"

"It's a Man's Job"

Women police officers? Lady firefighters? Mothers in politics? Heavens to Betsy!

In 1932, females in power were amusing or bizarre.

It's cliché to say the good old days were simpler times, but there's no chance a politically incorrect celebration like Leap Day would be considered today. Females in positions of authority have long stopped being rare. But when the tradition started, women had been voting for only twelve years, and asking whether a lady could actually run the city was considered a legitimate question, one the *Beacon-News* asked on February 29, 1932.

"Women are not suited for such work," John Hendrickson told the paper. "It's a man's job to handle the duties of a city official."

There's no word on what his mother said when she read that quote in the paper.

The Leap Day event was created as a fun break from the daily doldrums of the Great Depression.

Bachelors were rounded up and brought in front of the "powder puff council," where a twenty-two-year-old female police chief handed out tickets

Four women dressed as firefighters as part of the Leap Day festivities. *From the collection of the Aurora Historical Society.*

payable in five-pound boxes of candy. The men who resisted hid out in the smoke shop of Bud Santany, where the windows were marked "Custer's last stand. The hand that rocks the cradle doesn't rule here."

The 1932 city council finished its one-day term without enacting new laws, but Mayoress Mildred Pratt determined it was a "perfect" session since not a single tax dollar was spent. The idea that started on a lark sparked a tradition.

Store owners were quick to decide that Leap Day was the perfect opportunity for the most American of holiday institutions—a sale. On February 29, 1936, everything in the store was either $0.29, $1.29 or $2.29.

By then, Leap Day had taken off. Coverage in the *Beacon-News* mentions lipstick coppers fining bachelors in bon bons and silk lingerie. The faux city council passed a number of resolutions that year, then each member paused, took out a compact and powdered her nose to the delight of cameramen gathered at city hall to shoot newsreel footage.

"Being women, we expect to do things just a little bit better than they have ever done before," Mayor Esser Allen said in 1936.

Women dressed as firefighters as part of the Leap Day festivities. *From the collection of the Aurora Historical Society.*

Women firefighters were encouraged to powder up before going to a fire.

"Remember girls," Fire Chief Rosalie Smith warned, "you might meet a man at a fire. Be ready for anything."

In 1940, Kesel was the owner of Audre' Kesel's School of the Dance on South Broadway. She can't remember how she ever got mixed up in the Leap Day mayoral election, but her students and family members were suddenly sending in stacks of the ballots printed in the *Beacon-News*.

"I don't remember making speeches," she said. "I just remember saying, 'Oh hi, vote for me.' It was all just fun. Like a holiday."

She ended up beating four rivals and, at just twenty-one years old, she took her spot in the mayor's office. Her duties forced a change in her morning routine.

"I'm never one to get up and rush around," she said.

That day, her father scolded her, telling her the *Life Magazine* reporters and AP cameraman were all waiting. The highlights of her reign? She got to send a fire truck to Ogden Avenue to pick up her brother who was driving in from Chicago. And she got to eat dinner in the swanky Sky Club at the top of Leland Tower, where she sat next to the city's mayor the other 365 days.

"I was having trouble cutting my steak," she said, "and the mayor said, 'Let me help you.'"

At the end of the day, she went back to the dance studio. But Leap Day had a profound effect on her life.

An Out-of-Date Tradition

After a break for World War II in 1944, the Leap Day tradition continued. In 1948, Leap Day raised $125 for Hines Veterans Hospital. A Leap Day dance was added in 1952, where laughing bachelors paid fines in advance by purchasing tickets. In 1956, the 400 bachelors who were arrested raised $939 to be donated to the Heart Fund (although controversial Mayor Paul Egan caused headaches when he fired the Leap Day committee for not getting enough publicity).

The tradition continued until 1972, when women once again filled the city council with inane resolutions, including keeping a database with the names, ages and phone numbers of all eligible bachelors. But by then, women's roles had changed. Shirley Chisolm ran for president that year, and Frances Farenthold finished second on the ballot for vice president. Charlotte Reid had served five terms as Aurora's representative in the U.S. House. In just a few years, women would be on local school boards and city councils. Women in power was now a reality, not a novelty.

So it wasn't too surprising when the Women's Liberation Group of Aurora interrupted the Leap Day luncheon. Carrying three children, the women said the event was ridiculing single women and complained girls were being "duped" into taking part.

The event limped along for two more Leap Days, with waning interest and coverage. In 1984, Alderwoman Anne Baumann called it sexist. Leap Day's time was up.

But one lady never forgot her Leap Day experience. That good-looking young bachelor she sentenced to three pairs of nylons was Richard Grometer, Audre's future husband. They were married a few years after she finished her mayoral term.

"It was an exciting time that I lived in," Audre' Grometer said.

And what about now, where women are fire chiefs and mayors and may even be president? Grometer pumps her fist.

"Let's do it," she said, smiling.

Medal of Honor

It is insufficient to say the Medal of Honor is rare. Of the approximately 16 million men and women who served in the U.S. Armed Forces during World War II, just 464 earned the nation's highest military distinction. If you lined up everyone who served in the war, you would have to shake more than 3,300 soldiers' hands to have a chance at meeting a Medal of Honor recipient. It's more common for a baseball player to get an at-bat in the World Series. It's more likely you'll run into a Nobel Prize winner than a Medal of Honor recipient.

The Medal is bestowed upon soldiers for acts of selfless bravery. When we hear what these men have done, it seems impossible they are anything like us. We are ordinary.

So it is important to know that Walter Truemper was just a man. He didn't have superpowers. He went to East Aurora High School. He wrote home to his mother. He enjoyed a quiet game of cards.

But at the crucial moment, when his B-17 ran low on fuel and his commander ordered him to bail out, Truemper chose to stick by a helpless friend. Did his courage come from resolve? From stubbornness? Or was it from some place more gentle and sweet?

"WOULD NOT TRADE ONE MINUTE"

There wasn't much debate about whether or not to enlist. By 1942, all the young men were signing up, and every home seemed to have a blue star in the window. Two of Truemper's brothers were already overseas. Besides, the United States needed men like Walter Truemper.

Walter Truemper. Beacon-News *archives.*

After graduating from East Aurora High School, he worked at Aurora City Lines while taking night classes at Northwestern University. Although he had never been in a plane, it wasn't a big surprise that, five months after he enlisted, he was sent to aviation school. He was articulate, kind and had an easy brilliance with numbers. He could add long rows of numbers as easily as he could read a sentence.

The crowded barracks must have felt like home. Truemper was the eighth of ten children. His father manufactured cigars and had served as a city commissioner. Truemper loved and respected his father, but he had a special bond with his mother. While he was still in elementary school, his mother's arthritis became so severe that she couldn't walk. She refused a wheelchair, however, preferring to sit in a huge rocking chair where she enjoyed the activity in the house.

If her condition bothered her, Fredericka Truemper never let her children know. Until the day she died, she never complained. As the children did the household chores, she sang to them gently from upstairs.

Though Walter Truemper shot through the ranks, his heart was never far from Aurora. He wrote home nearly every day. And nearly every day, his sister Ann would write back on her mother's behalf, sharing news of family and friends. By May 1943, Truemper had no illusions about his future. Although he was still months from shipping out, the twenty-five year-old made sure he told his mother the impact she'd had on his life.

> *It takes times like these to show a person how much his mother really means to him. What this letter is trying to say is that I realize, and have always realized, what a wonderful mother I really have. If it were possible for me to be with you, it would be a simple matter for me to express myself. But as it is, words must suffice.*

I want to thank you for the countless hours you have spent worrying about my welfare, as well as the years spent raising me from childhood to the man I am today. My life has been such that I would not trade one minute of it for anything worldly.

Now I see that my duty is to see this war through to a most successful conclusion, so that in the days to come my life can be better for it. When we are together again, God willing, you will realize just how my feelings are towards you. If it is my lot to be one of those who suffer the extreme sacrifice, I will be proud to do it if our way of life will continue.

My reason for saying this is to let you know that it is possible that we may never meet again. If this is the case, I just want you to know that regardless of what happens, it is for the best. I wasn't going to mention this, but I might as well pour out everything in my heart.

May our Lord bestow his richest blessing upon you and keep you until the day when we can spend a memorable reunion day together.

With all my love, Mom.
Your boy,
Walter

OFF TO WAR AND INTO BATTLE

The boy who wrote home was also a man with a navigational gift. Although he had never flown on a plane before leaving home, Truemper's mathematical ability proved to be a natural fit for aviation.

Truemper was assigned to a crew of ten men from all over the country: Texas, New Jersey, North Dakota, Pennsylvania, Ohio, Washington and Illinois. The youngest was twenty-two; the oldest, twenty-seven. Despite their differences, they bonded around their plane, a B-17. The lumbering four-engine long-range bombers were often called "Flying Fortresses" because of the power they could pack on long flights. The 74-foot-long plane held 10 crew members: a pilot, co-pilot, navigator, radio operator and six gunners—all of whom also worked other jobs. Even loaded up and weighing 54,000 pounds, the plane could cruise at more than 180 miles per hour and drop 2,700 pounds of bombs.

The mother of one of the men in Truemper's crew had given the beastly plane the gentle nickname *Mizpah*, from Genesis 31:49: "And Mizpah; for he said, the Lord watch between me and thee, when we are absent from one another."

According to the book *Valor at Polebrook* by Jeff Rogers and Rick School, Truemper found his niche in this crew as a world-class navigator. When flying, he could tune the instrument panel to radio stations and then use the signals to find the plane's coordinates as it moved, a complicated but traditional navigation technique at the time. But on night flights, Truemper showed his true genius. Using a sextant and paper, he used the stars to calculate their location as they moved through the sky. Friends would bet him that he would miss a checkpoint by more than three minutes using celestial navigation. They never collected.

Were his friends exaggerating? In late 1943, he wrote home, asking his mother to sit in the southern window of the house around noon. To protect troop movements, soldiers weren't allowed to tell their families what day they would be leaving. But Truemper promised his mother if she sat at that window, she would know. He had calculated their flight from Nebraska to New York would pass over Aurora, or at least close enough for a slight detour.

On the afternoon of November 30, as Fredericka Truemper sat near the window, a shadow dashed across the backyard before briefly passing over the picture window. A few minutes later, the plane's shadow again moved across Fredericka's lap.

Walter Truemper, the navigator who never missed, had waved goodbye to his mother. He was going to war.

The crew of the *Mizpah* arrived at the Polebrook airfield in December 1943, probably a few weeks after Captain Clark Gable finished five missions that were filmed for an educational series on the Royal Air Force. For months, Truemper and his men waited in dreary central England. In mid-February, they flew a training flight. It was a last check of planes before one of the biggest raids in air force history.

The mission was, at the time, an unprecedented airstrike against the Nazis. More than two thousand Allied heavy bombers and long-range fighters would fly into Germany, targeting fighter plane factories in Leipzig, Gotha, Bernberg, Oschersieben, Brunswick and Halberstadt. Each plane had its role, one silver bee in a swarm of planes that would fly for hours while exposed to air and ground fire. *Mizpah* lifted off around 9:40 a.m. on February 20, one of sixteen planes from the 351st bomb squadron flying in formation. As they crossed the silent, empty English Channel, the men made their flight checks and waited.

Almost as soon as *Mizpah* entered German air space, Nazi planes darted out of the clouds, spraying bullets and firing shells. Then, silence. The men scanned the skies for the next attack.

Around 1:30 p.m., two Nazi fighters began firing on *Mizpah*. The pilot's overhead window exploded, killing co-pilot Ronald Bartley instantly. The other pilot, Lieutenant Richard Nelson, slumped forward, still strapped to his seat.

What was left of Bartley's body leaned on the plane's control, forcing it into a steep dive. Alarm bells sounded, and the freezing wind rushed through the window. As it dove, *Mizpah* began to spin, pinning the crew against the wall and increasing the chaos.

"It felt like my eyeballs were going to pop out through my cheekbones," a crew member recalled.

The plane spun wildly as it dropped fifteen thousand feet until, incredibly, crew member Carl Moore forced himself into a space between the two pilots and grabbed the controls. According to Rogers and School, Moore used his elbows to push the pilots off the controls and then yanked the plane back into steady flight.

Second Lieutenant Walter Truemper was now the ranking officer on the flight. They were over enemy territory, flying a wounded plane. One pilot was dead and the other, Lieutenant Nelson, was probably dying. Archie Mathies, a twenty-six-year-old Pennsylvania coal miner, took over flying. Truemper went below and tried to calculate where they had been hit, how far they had gone off course and which way was toward home base.

At home in Aurora, Fredericka Truemper was uneasy. The night before, she had had a dream that bothered her.

"Something has happened to Walter," she told the family.

STILL BREATHING

For three hours, Mathies and Truemper, two relatively inexperienced pilots, rotated flying duties. The wind blasted through the open window, numbing their hands and faces. Some of the surviving crew members had been seriously injured. Numbed by morphine, they braced for more attacks.

Around 3:30 p.m. the *Mizpah* broke through the clouds over England. By then, the men had been in the air for six hours. They were tired, injured and shaken. And yet the biggest challenge lay ahead. While navigating home was a challenge, controlling the plane had been relatively easy: set an altitude and point the beast west. Landing, however, was another matter.

The airfield at Polebrook had three runways, each a little more than 1,100 yards long. Truemper and Mathies had decided Mathies could land the

Archie Mathies. *Library of Congress.*

plane. Truemper got on the headset to relay messages to and from the tower. As they approached, Mathies flipped the landing gear switch. The plane descended, but it was coming in too quickly at nearly 160 miles per hour.

According to Rogers and School, the men aboard the *Mizpah* didn't believe the plane would land smoothly. They figured it might hit the grass and slide along on its belly. In that scenario, if just the tip of a wing clipped the ground, the plane would flip and rip into pieces. Survival was 50–50.

At nearly the last moment, Mathies pulled *Mizpah* up. On the ground, the radio tower crew watched as the plane surged back into the sky and began to circle. The order to abandon ship came through.

With Mathies holding the plane as steady as possible, Joe Rex, followed by Russell Robinson, Mac Hogbo and Tom Sowell leapt to safety. Moore was the last to leap. He shook hands with Mathies and Truemper, said a prayer for his friends and then jumped. All of these men would survive and be awarded Purple Hearts. They would go on to get married, run businesses, start families.

But Mathies and Truemper were now on their own.

The plane was scarred with bullet holes and dented by cannon strikes. Mathies tried to bring the plane in again, only to pull up short when the plane was coming in too fast.

It had been an hour since *Mizpah* had first approached Polebrook Field. Fuel was running low, and other planes were due to return from what had been an incredibly successful mission. Decisions had to be made. The ground crew no longer believed that Truemper and Mathies could slow the plane enough for a landing. So a new order came in: aim the plane toward the Atlantic, set it on autopilot and bail out.

There was a pause. The ground crew waited for a response.

Inside *Mizpah*, Truemper and Mathies considered their options. Nelson's face was bleeding from the shrapnel that had burst through the windshield.

He was helpless, imprisoned in a seat that would not release him. But he was alive.

Truemper finally replied to the bail-out order.

"Sir, if that's an order, OK," Truemper told the ground crew. "But we'd rather try to bring her in. The pilot is still breathing."

FIVE MONTHS LATER

Fredericka Truemper's two oldest sons carried their mother to the front lawn. She was in her large rocking chair, still helpless, imprisoned by a disease that would not release her.

The men placed the large rocking chair under a giant oak tree. Her hands were folded gently on her lap. Her son's silver wings shone on her black dress.

Fredericka Truemper receiving the Medal of Honor from Brigadier General of the United States Army R.E. O'Neill at a ceremony on the front lawn of the family's home at 807 North Avenue. *Courtesy of Ann Prestero.*

Normally, the Medal of Honor was presented in Washington, D.C., by the President of the United States. But due to Fredericka's condition, the Air Force had agreed to come to Aurora.

As people wept around her, Fredericka listened to the brigadier general of the United States Army read a citation awarding the Medal of Honor to her son, Second Lieutenant Walter E. Truemper.

"For conspicuous gallantry and intrepidity at risk of life above beyond the call of duty in action against the enemy," General R.E. O'Neill read.

Fredericka's head bowed slightly. Her eyes filled with tears. Later, they would name a street, bridges, post offices and military bases after both Walter Truemper and Archibald Mathies. The citizens of Aurora would dedicate a monument at the city's beautiful sunken garden. Although her faith told her that her son was in a better place, Fredericka would never get over his death.

"Demonstrating unsurpassed courage and heroism," O'Neill continued, "Second Lt. Truemper and the engineer replied that the pilot was still alive but could not be moved, and they would not desert him. They were then told to attempt a landing. After two unsuccessful efforts, their plane crashed into an open field in a third attempt to land. Second Lieutenant Truemper, the engineer and the wounded pilot were killed."

General O'Neill leaned forward with the medal. Fredericka Truemper smiled, raised her head and accepted the nation's highest military honor on behalf of her son.

Monument honoring Medal of Honor recipient Walter Truemper, an Aurora native. *Photo by Matt Hanley.*

From Boxcars to Bears

They waited more than two hours to pay their respects. The line of mourners stretched out of Daleiden Funeral Home, down Cedar Street, around the corner to Wilder and then down two more blocks to New York Street. Politicians and policemen, judges and junkies, mayors and military men, the powerful and penniless stood in line on an unusually warm day in February 1999. Visitation was scheduled for seven hours but had to be extended to accommodate the crowd.

Pete Perez had made a difference. The line at his wake was tangible evidence of that. He had been a Chicago Bear, a champion weightlifter, a legendary police officer and a hero to little boys all over the city. But most of all, he was Uncle Pete, the compassionate cop with the big heart.

During his thirty-four years in law enforcement, he had seen the worst. His first beat was skid row, where drunks stabbed each other between rounds. He had tried to help drug-addicted kids living in neglectful squalor. It was a career that would have left many officers justifiably cynical and world weary. But Perez never lost his big laugh and easy smile. To him, life was not tragic; it was full of wonderful opportunities. His own story was proof of that.

El Scrape

Mexican President Porfirio Diaz turned back a French invasion, became a peacetime president and built a railway system that modernized his country. Then Diaz became a corrupt old man, rigging elections in his favor and sparking the Mexican Revolution.

Like all uprisings, the revolution had many terrible battles, as well as thousands of tiny clashes in towns, in neighborhoods and in men's consciences.

For instance, there was the day around 1910 when government troops rode onto Manuel Perez's land. According to research by Aurora University professor Susan Palmer, the troops let their horses loose in Perez's fields. The animals trampled the family's corn, wiping out months of work.

Disgusted, Manuel Perez joined the rebellion. But he couldn't stomach raiding the homes of former neighbors. So when he quit the rebels, Manuel Perez became an enemy of both sides. He escaped by burying himself, his wife and his young son in a wagonload of hay headed for Northern Mexico. Manuel Perez found work in a border factory and dreamed of moving to the United States. The Chicago, Burlington & Quincy Railroad provided the means.

By the 1920s, the CB&Q Railroad had an incredible network of rail lines—twelve thousand miles of track across fourteen states. And the company was so desperate for help, they would pay the moving expenses of laborers willing to go to Aurora, Illinois. The work was tough. Men cut up engines with torches and hammers, so the parts could be reused. But the wages were decent, and the Perezes found there was another perk. Workers had convinced the railroad to allow them to live in abandoned boxcars for almost nothing.

Soon, in a dirt field just east of the city, two dozen cars were lined up parallel to the tracks. With the wheels removed, each family lived in a car about eleven feet wide and thirty feet long. In most cars, a bed sheet divided the bedrooms from the kitchen. There was no running water, no electricity and no plumbing. The walls were thin and the stoves were weak, but the bonds were strong. When the Depression and discrimination drove thousands of Mexicans back to their native land, the population of *El Scrape* (the Scrapyard) grew to three hundred Mexican immigrants. The isolated cars became a community. Men and women would dance in Phillip's Park and listen to the music of their home country. They saved their money. They built a chapel from parts of train cars. Every week, a man from Chicago brought in beans and tortillas.

"It wasn't the Hilton Hotel, obviously, but what else could you ask for during the Depression?" Ralph Cruz, one of the original residents told the *Beacon-News* in 2005. "We had everything—a job, no rent, free food. Here, we were like kings."

The children climbed the boxcars, shot marbles, spun tops, swatted dragonflies with baseball bats and stuck pennies on the railroad tracks. Unlike

The Perez family. Pete Perez is sitting in the middle of the bottom row. *Courtesy of the Perez family.*

their parents, they could not ignore the rest of the world. They were sent into Aurora's schools, where they usually faced incomprehensible classes.

In 1924, Manuel Perez's sixth son, Pete, was born into this world. Manuel had gotten a job with CB&Q Railroad and moved into Boxcar No. 15. Pete Perez spent his first eight years crammed in an abandoned boxcar. He never stopped being proud of that.

PLAYING IN THE PROS

On September 28, 1945, the Chicago Bears ran through one last three-hour practice at St. Joseph College in Indiana. It was a rainy day, and the squad undoubtedly let their minds wander to next week's opener against Curly Lambeau's Green Bay Packers.

Like most NFL teams at the time, the rosters were in a bit of disarray. The Bears still had future Hall of Famer Sid Luckman as quarterback, but the military draft had grabbed other talent, including all-pro center Bulldog

Turner and running back George McAfee. Even head coach and team founder George Halas had been called to the navy, leaving the Bears with co-head coaches to guide them through their last drill before opening day.

In the middle of the scrimmage was number 19, a quick, strong twenty-one-year-old guard from Aurora, Illinois, who was 5'9" and weighed 220 pounds. The boy born in a tiny boxcar was now a giant. Pete Perez was a professional football player and was paid $150 per game. With curly black hair that sometimes fell over his forehead, Perez stood out for more than just his strength. In 1945, there were no black players in the NFL and only a handful of Hispanic players.

Being an outsider was nothing new. By 1934, El Scrape was abandoned. The families who lived there moved into or built homes in the city. Cruz, Perez, Salazar, Vera, Nila and Godinez—names that would fill city ledgers for the next century—mixed into neighborhoods that had been solidly Romanian, German, Irish and Luxembourgian for decades. Like most immigrants, the parents were able to cling to their traditions, but their children were forced to find some middle ground between their heritage and their new home.

"We came out and became part of the community," Pete Perez would later say. "We just about forced them to like us, or at least accept the contributions we'd made."

Perez made the most of it. He excelled in school and was a stand-out lineman at Marmion Military Academy, a Catholic, all-boys high school. He earned a full athletic scholarship to play offensive tackle at the University of Illinois. During World War II, Perez left school to join the military, but a perforated eardrum sent him to the Merchant Marines. When

Pete Perez in uniform for the Chicago Bears. *Courtesy of the Perez family.*

he finished his service, he was eligible to return to Champaign. But after just one year of college, Perez convinced Illini coach Ray Elliott to help him catch on with the Bears.

The season Perez played for the Bears, the team finished 3–7 while playing at Wrigley Field. Perez saw action in three games against the Packers, Cleveland Rams and Chicago Cardinals. The next year, when many starters returned from the service, Perez was on the outside. He continued to play minor league football, lining up for the Akron Bears and the Bethlehem (PA) Bulldogs. For the 1950 season, he had a good offer from a Canadian football league. But Perez was twenty-six and tired of "being a traveling vagabond". (Besides, he had already gotten his ring—he married Marie, the prettiest fan of the Bulldogs, that year.) Perez decided to return to his roots. He found a job with the CB&Q Railroad, the company that had brought his father to Aurora.

He had been a college football star and groundbreaking professional player, but Pete Perez's greatest accomplishments were still ahead of him.

Uncle Pete

Hector Jordan and Pete Perez comprised the entire Hispanic population in the Aurora Police Department in 1958. Jordan was the first, hired in 1956. At his interview, Jordan was told he was being hired to patrol the Hispanic population. When he scoffed at the insult, the department backed off. Two years later, Jordan recruited Perez to join him.

Perez's first assignment was walking Aurora's skid row. For ten years, he dealt with drunks pouring out of bars and knife-fighting in street. In football, Perez had been an undersized lineman. On the streets of Aurora, his imposing figure prompted strangers to approach him and say they had heard he was the toughest guy in town and challenge him to a fight.

Perez could handle himself in a scuffle, but he always preferred a smile and a talk. He laughed, a big towering burst of happiness that filled a room. He and Jordan, who became as close as brothers, were the department's practical jokers.

"Pete was a guy that loved everybody, and everybody loved him. Everyone that crossed paths with him became his friend," said former Aurora Police Chief Robert Brent. "But all he had to do was bark, and it was all over."

On Brent's first day, he was assigned to work with Perez. Brent watched Perez's genuine affection for people. He treated dignitaries and derelicts all the same. Even years later, when he was named chief, Brent would find himself wondering how Pete Perez would handle the situation he himself was facing. What would he say?

After walking the beat, Perez was moved to investigations. Slowly, some of the pioneering officers left the department. Jordan, who felt he was unable to advance due to his race, joined the Federal Bureau of Narcotics and Dangerous Drugs, where he became one of the nation's top undercover agents. Clinton Mayes, Aurora's first black officer, left to become a decorated patrolman with the state police. But Perez stayed. In 1966, he was named Police Officer of the Year. The next year, he was assigned to help create the department's juvenile division. Not surprisingly, he found common ground with young people who came from tough circumstances. Compassion came naturally. He became "Uncle Pete" to hundreds of young people. He would give them football tips or offer a lesson on the finer points of parking lot baseball. He would invite young persons to lift weights with him so they had somewhere to go and something to do.

In 1967, Kane County Youth Home Superintendent Marlan Tevis wrote, "In this day and age in which there seems to be so much disregard for authority and especially for police officers, it certainly is unusual when youngsters who come to the youth home and are confined here will indicate Pete Perez is one of the best friends they have."

After twenty-one years with the Aurora Police, Perez could have retired in 1979. Instead, at fifty-four, he moved to the Kane County Sheriff's Department, where he was named second in command. He worked for the county another thirteen years before retiring.

After he retired, the city named a street and a Hispanic Heritage Award after Pete Perez. The man born on the margins had redrawn the lines.

"His story is a story that every Hispanic in Aurora should know," said former Aurora Commander Michael Nila, who also spent his first day as an Aurora officer with Perez. "In his story, everyone can find something to be inspired by."

Pete Perez died at age seventy-four in Aurora, not far from the boxcar community where he was born. There were hundreds of people whose lives were better because of him, including his six children, who found warmth in their father's substantial shadow. They had become teachers, corporate vice presidents, sheriffs, firemen, bank executives and policemen. They knew their father's reputation but were overwhelmed at his wake when stranger after stranger shared personal stories. Pete got me into rehab, they said. Pete saved my life. Pete helped my son. Pete listened. Pete was a friend.

At one point, Pete's son Pat Perez walked his sons down the long line of mourners. The boys were still too young to appreciate all their grandfather had overcome and all that he had accomplished, but they needed to see these people.

"This is what a great man your grandfather was," Pat Perez told his sons. "This is what we all have to live up to."

Kennedy and Nixon

After all the debates, campaign stickers, electorate polls, conventions, TV commercials, newspaper editorials, small-town parades and political speeches, the presidential election of 1960 was decided by 112,827 votes. That's less than one-tenth of a percent of the 68.3 million votes cast. When you look at it from that angle, every stop on the campaign trail was crucial. Any visit may have been the tipping point.

That being said, history has not assigned any great significance to the fact that in 1960, John F. Kennedy (on October 25) and Richard Nixon (on October 29) came to Fox Valley. They did not deliver any unforgettable, ask-not-what-your-country-can-do speeches while they were here. They did not make bold changes in strategy during their visits.

They moved through these towns in a rush. Aurora and Wheaton must have seemed like a hundred other towns they had seen since the nomination.

The true impact was on the residents. They would never forget their brush with these great men. How could they? Kennedy and Nixon were here during the final days of an unprecedented campaign. These men were debating the ideas that would shape the country and doing it on live television.

An estimated 70 million viewers watched the first debate, which even then was famous because Nixon allegedly looked tired and pale on TV but sounded fine on the radio. The next three debates were blockbusters. Nixon called Kennedy immature, rash and unsophisticated.

"Senator Kennedy's call for U.S. government support of a revolution in Cuba is the most shockingly reckless proposal ever made in our history by a presidential candidate during a campaign," Nixon said. Kennedy faulted the

Republicans for trying to wreck Social Security and opposing what would become Medicaid.

"Let me make it perfectly clear that I have always opposed socialized medicine—what the Republicans really oppose is adequate care," Kennedy said. "In 1933, they pretended that Social Security would Sovietize America. Did it?"

As often happens in close presidential races, the country's future seemed to hang in the balance, so people wanted to have a say. More than half of Aurora's population registered to vote, a thousand more than in the last presidential election. In Kane County, there were ten thousand new voters registered. Illinois's twenty-seven electoral votes seemed within the grasp of both candidates, so with weeks to go, they set their eyes on the Land of Lincoln.

Nixon would speak at Wheaton College. After landing at O'Hare at 9:20 a.m., Kennedy planned stops in Libertyville, Barrington, Carpentersville and Elgin, followed by a brief stop for lunch and rest at Hotel Baker in St. Charles and then on to Geneva, Batavia, Mooseheart and Aurora by 3:30 p.m.

The October 26, 1960 *Beacon-News* reported:

> *In Libertyville, Barrington, Meadowdale, Elgin, St. Charles, Batavia, men, women and children pressed against the Senator's car, their hands outstretched or yelling for autographs. Kennedy's response was the shaking of as many hands as possible, a word or two where it could be heard.*
>
> *As Kennedy moved deeper into Kane County, the number of Nixon posters and Republican banners waved by roadside supporters increased.*
>
> *A crowd estimated at between 3,500 and 5,000 people gathered at Baker Park. Senator Kennedy and his entourage of about 180 were nearly an hour late arriving in St. Charles but it was a beautiful day and there were the hucksters with campaign hats, buttons and banners and other interesting things to pass the time. James Broglin of St. Charles brought his little gray mule all dressed up for the occasion. He had the letters J F K on his sides with adhesive tape and wore a Kennedy hat with his huge ears sticking through.*

TOM

Tom was ten years old and living in Batavia. He liked the Chicago Cubs and the Three Stooges.

One day in October, with nothing much else going on, Tom, his nine-year-old neighbor and his neighbor's mom walked three blocks for a chance to see John F. Kennedy. They stood on the lawn of a funeral home, stretching to get a look. People were everywhere.

Tom had heard about Kennedy. His dad, a moderate Republican, watched the debates and was impressed.

Tom was curious to see the guy that had been on TV. Sure, Kennedy was no Ernie Banks, but Tom was ten and everything was interesting. Even though the adults said Kennedy wasn't going to stop in Batavia, he did. He was like a giant in that great big car.

Kennedy talked for a little while about things that didn't matter much to a kid. But Tom thought, "I like this guy. He seems like he knows what he's talking about."

Tom later became a Democrat, joined the Peace Corps and even became mayor of Aurora. And while it would make a nice story to say that all started that day in Batavia, that's not the case.

But John F. Kennedy left an impression. And Tom Weisner would always be glad he got a chance to see him. Even if he was no Ernie Banks.

John F. Kennedy in Aurora. *From the collection of the Aurora Historical Society.*

Sen. John F. Kennedy, his brown hair flecked with confetti, stood on the steps of Aurora's city hall yesterday and charged U.S. prestige has fallen.

Before him stood a cheering, screaming crowd estimated at from 12,000 to 15,000 persons. The crowd, which contained numerous children, stretched east and west of city hall, jammed itself from sidewalk to sidewalk and surged back and forth as Kennedy approached and spoke.

Limiting his appearance to approximately eight minutes, because the motorcade was running 45 minutes late, Kennedy pointed to international relations with Russia, Africa and the Far East, the Berlin situations, national defense and employment as problems which will face the next president.

WILMA

When Wilma Howard, forty-one, heard that John F. Kennedy would be speaking at city hall in downtown Aurora, she knew just what to do. She went down to the drug store and got a cowbell. She did it for the same reason she had pinned a Kennedy sign on the back of her Boston terrier and marched him up and down the street. This was a great, great man, and everybody needed to know.

When Wilma reached downtown, the streets were packed. She almost had her arm around the guy next to her and she couldn't even put the cowbell down. There was no room.

She loved that day and loved Kennedy. For the rest of her life, she would read everything she could find about the Kennedys until she finally had to donate a box of books to the library because her husband couldn't stand it anymore. She never got rid of that cowbell, though.

As he pressed through the corridor of Aurora's crowded city hall, Kennedy emerged onto the speaker's platform in a gentle rain. As the crowd howled and front row fans threw confetti, Kennedy shook hands with those near enough.

Standing without a raincoat, Kennedy said: "The Bible tells us it rains on the just and the unjust and I know there are a few Republicans out there so they're getting wet, too."

JEAN

Jean Jackson, twenty-four years old, set out for downtown Aurora, carrying her two-year-old son, holding the hand of her three-year-old son and hauling an umbrella.

At home, they had a big picture of Kennedy hanging in the house. She talked to the boys and told them what a great man he was. She wanted the boys to see this man.

That day, they stood at the back of the crowd, barely getting a glimpse of the candidate. But they heard him say something about the rain falling on rich and poor. Jean liked that.

As she stood there carrying one son, holding the other's hand and clutching the umbrella, she was so happy she had brought the boys.

"I just wish I had pictures," she'd say later. "I couldn't carry a camera."

Pausing after the close of his brief speech to shake more hands, Kennedy retired to a washroom while police formed a cordon, paused to let a photographer take a picture, asked for a Coke and left when he found out it would take too long to secure the soft drink.

His convertible was drawn up against the east side of city hall. Fourteen fireman and two police shifts worked to restrain frenzied well-wishers and 24 Red Cross volunteers stood by.

KATHLEEN

Kathleen Kort was twelve years old, fascinated by politics and an ardent supporter of her guy, John F. Kennedy. When Kennedy came to Aurora, they listened to his speech on the radio at her home on the outskirts of Aurora. Kathleen was enthralled. And she had a plan.

If they left now, they might be able to see his car drive by. She begged her dad to please, please, please take her to where the motorcade would pass. But Kort's dad wasn't all that enthusiastic about politics. He was even less enthusiastic about seeing politicians drive by in the rain.

But his little girl wanted to go. So they hopped in the car, drove to a spot on the motorcade route and scrambled out to wait on the side of the road.

And just as Kennedy drove by, Kort's dad (and this was the kind of thing he would always do) yelled out, "Hey, over here!"

Kennedy and Nixon

Democratic presidential candidate John F. Kennedy receiving the key to the city from Aurora Mayor Paul Egan. *From the collection of the Aurora Historical Society.*

And wouldn't you know it? John F. Kennedy turned and waved right at their family. What a great guy.

> *With a blue Illinois sky for his background and 32,000 roaring Republicans for his audience, Richard Millhouse Nixon, the vice president of the United States and the man who wants to be president, entered Wheaton Sunday.*
>
> *Facing a vigorously responsive crowd, Nixon quashed recession talk by his opponent John F. Kennedy, said America is the greatest country in the world today and referred again and again to the rights of the individual in America.*
>
> *The spectacle was complete with two bands, lost children, a man who lost both sets of car keys and a monumental traffic jam as persons sought to see the candidate off and return to their cars.*

POSTSCRIPT

On October 25, 1960, Democratic nominee John F. Kennedy swept through Geneva, St. Charles, Batavia and Aurora, making speeches to thousands of people. Four days later, Vice President and Republican nominee Richard Nixon spoke to thousands of people in Wheaton.

Those that were there saved photos, pins and newspaper clippings of the young Massachusetts senator's stop. He was so handsome, they said. He didn't need a microphone. His voice carried perfectly, hitting each ear at just the right volume. He shook hands with everyone. When the *Beacon-News* asked readers to send in memories on the fiftieth anniversary, dozens of Kennedy stories came in. But not a single Nixon memory.

In retellings, people remember Kennedy's visit as transformational. For some, it made them think about politics for the first time.

Here are the facts behind those memories: Kennedy lost the Fox Valley. He was trounced.

In Aurora, he won just 17 of 58 precincts and lost the city by 3,500 votes. He lost Kane County by 24,000 votes. He lost in the cities and in the rural areas. He lost Batavia, Geneva, St. Charles, Elgin, Sugar Grove...and so on.

What accounts for the disconnect between what happened and how people remember it?

Maybe it is revisionist history. Maybe the election was a cultural turning point for this area, even if the results didn't yet show it. Maybe the people enamored with Kennedy's visit were younger, so they were still alive to share their stories five decades later.

No matter the results, the truth is that Kennedy and Nixon made a lasting impression.

All excerpts in this chapter come from *Beacon-News* articles dated October 26–30, 1960.

Bibliography

The following stories were previously in the *Beacon-News* and are adapted here with permission: The Wright Stuff (June 29, 2010), Leap-Year Ladies (February 29, 2008), Abraham Lincoln and the Aurora Water Wheel Case (February 17, 2008 and March 2, 2008), On the Trail of a Killer (May 13–19, 2007), Founding Brothers (April 30, 2009 and July 22, 2010), A City of Lights (December 21, 2008), In the Line of Duty (May 14–19, 2006), Two Burials of Three-Fingered Hamilton (October 31, 2010).

FOUNDING BROTHERS

This story was built from contributions by Aurora Historical Society executive director John Jaros and the microfiche archives of the Aurora *Beacon-News*, as cited in the story.

ABRAHAM LINCOLN AND THE AURORA WATER WHEEL CASE

The original case file for Hoyt v. Parker was destroyed in the Great Chicago Fire. Goodrich's recollections about the water wheel suit come from the book *Herndon's Lincoln: The True Story of a Great Life and Personal Recollections of Abraham Lincoln*. The timeline for the story was built from the wonderful website thelincolnlog.org. The information about Goodrich leaving the case comes from www.lawpracticeofabrahamlincoln.org, a treasure-trove of primary source Lincoln law documents. Finally, the background about Hoyt came from a *Beacon-News* obituary. Aurora Historical Society Executive Director John Jaros provided important background context for Aurora in the 1850s, and John Lupton, the associate director of the Papers of Abraham Lincoln in Springfield, provided vital details about the mechanics of the patent case.

Beacon-News. "Hoyt vs. Parker." July 18, 1850.
———. "The United States Circuit Court." August 8, 1850.
Benner, Martha L., et al., eds. *The Law Practice of Abraham Lincoln: Complete Documentary Edition.* 2nd ed. Springfield: Illinois Historic Preservation Agency, 2009. http://www.lawpracticeofabrahamlincoln.org.
Herndon, William Henry. *Herndon's Lincoln: The True Story of a Great Life and Personal Recollections of Abraham Lincoln.* Springfield, IL: Herndon's Lincoln Publishing, 1909. http://archive.org/details/herndonslincolnt02herndon
The Lincoln Log: A Daily Chronology of the Life of Abraham Lincoln. Last modified 2012. http:// www.thelincolnlog.org.

A City of Lights

All stories about the competition between the East Side and West Side merchants came from *Beacon-News* articles published in 1908. Aurora Historical Society Executive Director John Jaros explained the early history of Aurora's business climate.

The Wright Stuff

The bulk of this story, including all anecdotes about the Wright Brothers' flight in Aurora, was taken from stories printed in the *Beacon-News*. The state of the Wright Brothers' business when they arrived in Aurora came from the book *The Bishop's Boys* by Tom Crouch. Although the Aurora flights are often cited as the first flight in Illinois, the *Chicago Tribune* made note of other flights in Hawthorne Park a few days before the Wright plane few in Aurora.

Beacon-News. "Aeroplane in Pretty Flight." July 7, 1910.
———. "Airship Goes Up Tonight." July 6, 1910.

———. "An Aeroplane Costs Money." June 4, 1910.

———. "An Aeroplane Is Not A Toy." June 27, 1910.

———. "Aurora Fans Are Betting on Flight." July 2, 1910.

———. "Aurora Men Meet Wright." June 3, 1910.

———. "Aurora Ship High in Air." June 28, 1910.

———. "Deal Closed for Airships." June 16, 1910.

———. "Giving Away Air." July 11, 1910.

———. "Great Homecoming Celebration Begins Tomorrow." July 1, 1910.

———. "New Airship for Aurora." June 24, 1910.

———. "No Horses at Driving Park." June 25, 1910.

———. "Several Wagons to Haul Airship." June 22, 1910.

———. "Statement by Mr. Russell, Manager for the Wright Brothers." July 5, 1910.

———. "Wind Checks Are the Rule." July 5, 1910.

———. "Wright Aeroplanes Arrive in Aurora: One Put on Parade." July 2, 1910.

———. "Won't Fly on Sunday." June 18, 1910.

Burton, Charles Pierce, "Now and Then," July 6, 1941.

Chicago Tribune. "Aviator Drops 800 Ft.; Lives." July 6, 1910.

———."Wright Plane Flies in Aurora." July 3, 1910.

Crouch, Tom. *The Bishop's Boys: A Life of Orville and Wilbur Wright.* New York: W.W. Norton, 2003.

CASEY AT THE MOLAR

The bulk of the story was built from *Beacon-News* stories. Stengel's statistics and some facts about the Wisconsin-Illinois League are from baseball-reference.com. The Polo Grounds anecdote and dentistry quote come from Chicago Tribune articles. *Stengel: His Life and Times* by Robert Creamer provided context on Stengel's career and the minor league system. All the colorful anecdotes about Stengel's time in Aurora are from Stengel's circuitous autobiography. Larry Sutton's scouting report came from "Baseball's Greatest Quotations" by Paul Dickson.

Beacon-News. "Albert Tebeau, Former Aurora Manager, Dies." March 14, 1944.

———. "Blues Drop Game 5-2." April 26, 1911.

———. "Blues Lose a Forfeit Game." September 6, 1911.

———. "Booster Day August 30." August 28, 1911.

———. "Both Games to Aurora." August 12, 1911.

———. "Brooklyn Gets Aurora Players." September 1, 1911.

———. "'Casey' Stengel, Former Aurora Fielder, World Series Hero." October 11, 1923.

———. "Expect Crowd At First Game." May 2, 1911.

———. "Fond du Lac Quits the W-I League." July 27, 1911.

———. "Former Blue Makes Good." September 8, 1912.

———. "Game recaps and box scores." April 14, 1911–September 13, 1911.

———. "Heard Around the W.-I. Circuit." July 13, 1911.

———. "New Uniforms For The 'Blues'." April 4, 1911.

———. "Season To Be Big One." April 24, 1911.

———. "Tebeau Quits Aurora Club." July 29, 1911.

———. "W-I Clubs Are Ready." May 1, 1911.

———. "Will Start With $3,500." March 23, 1911.

———. "Wisconsin-Illinois League." November 4, 1911.

"Casey Stengel Managerial Record." Last modified 2012. http://www.baseball-reference.com/managers/stengca01.shtml

"Casey Stengel Player Page." Last modified 2012. http://www.baseball-reference.com/managers/stengca01.shtml

Chicago Tribune. "How Casey Got That Way." April 7, 1957.

———. "In the Wake of the News." September 13, 1952.

———. "In the Wake of the News." March 16, 1956.

———. "In the Wake of the News." September 12, 1958.

———. "Old Timers Frolic, Spin Yarns of Days Gone By." June 23, 1963.

Creamer, Robert. Stengel: His Life and Times. Lincoln: University of Nebraska Press, 1996.

Dickson, Paul. Baseball's Greatest Quotations. New York: HarpersResource, 1992.

Stengel, Casey. Casey at the Bat: The Story of My Life in Baseball as told to Harry T. Paxton. New York: Random House, 1962.

IN THE LINE OF DUTY

This story was constructed entirely from *Beacon-News* and *Chicago Tribune* articles published from 1918 to 1933.

Beacon-News. "'All a Mistake' Says Stevens." June 15, 1919.
————. "City Council Offers Reward." November 3, 1918.
————. "Claim Stevens Had a Disguise." April 10, 1920.
————. "Gunmen Shoot Policemen." October 29, 1918.
————. "'He is the Man Who Shot Olin.'" June 13, 1919.
————. "Indicts Youth for Slaying of Police Officer." May 28, 1928.
————. "Killer of Policeman Gets Life." May 31, 1928.
————. "Murder Charge to Be Placed Against Boys." April 19, 1928.
————. "Murderers of Olin Are Known." October 30, 1918.
————. "Olin Expected Some Danger." October 31, 1918.
————. "Olin Slayer Still at Large." November 1, 1918.
————. "Policeman, Bandit Shoot It Out." April 16, 1928.
————. "Wounded Officer Quits Hospital." November 2, 1918.
————. "Says of Stevens: 'He Is the Man.'" June 12, 1919.
————. "Sensation as Case Ends." June 17, 1919.
————. "Stevens Asks Murder Trial." February 8, 1919.
————. "Stevens Defense Again Is on Alibi." April 9, 1920.
————. "Stevens Freed, Is Rearrested." June 18, 1919.
————. "Stevens Leaves Prison, Is Re-Arrested." January 28, 1925.
————. "Stevens Still Roams at Will." February 10, 1919.
————. "Stevens to Be Arrested as He Leaves Prison." January 23, 1925.
————. "Thousands Pay Final Tribute to Richardson." April 21, 1928.
————. "To Ask Death For Stevens." June 9, 1919.
————. "T. Richardson, Police Officer, Dies of Wound." April 18, 1928.
————. "Wounded Youth In Confession, Pal Arrested." April 17, 1928.
Chicago Tribune. "Alleged Police Slayer Caught After 14 Years." January 1, 1933.
————. "Aurora Cop Near Death After Battle With Youth." April 17, 1928.
————. "Extradition of Stevens Up to Governor Small." October 26, 1923.
————. "Gunman's Good Luck Changes." February 16, 1921.
————. "Out of $25,000 Bond, Seized as Suspected Slayer." May 22, 1919.
————. "Pardon Board Delays Action in Stevens Case." November 17, 1922.
————. "Police Seek 2 Chicagoans in Aurora Murder." October 30, 1918.
————. "Renew Assaults on Working Men." May 26, 1911.
————. "Stevens Balks at Extradition to Joliet Cell." October 28, 1923.
————. "Stevens Freed of Murder of Aurora Officer." June 18, 1919.
————. "Supreme Court Orders Stevens To Penitentiary." November 26, 1922.
————. "Walter Stevens, Dean of Gunmen, Dies." February 16, 1931.
————. "Walter Stevens, Hunted Over Year, Gives Self Up." February 8, 1919.
————. "Youth Given Life For Murder of Policeman." June 2, 1928.

ON THE TRAIL OF A KILLER

The stories were compiled mainly from *Beacon-News* stories published between April 23, 1923, and August 12, 1941. The *Chicago Tribune* archives (1923–26) also supplied supporting details. The skywriting details came in part from *America's Greatest Brands* newsletter. Warren Lincoln's relationship to the famous president and the background on Warren Lincoln's pre-Aurora life come from *For the People*, the newsletter of the Abraham Lincoln Association. Some details about what was found in Lincoln's house came from the July 1929 edition of *True Detective Stories*, written by Merlin Moore Taylor. A copy of *Silent, White and Beautiful* was supplied by the Aurora Historical Society. A copy of Michels's scrapbook in the Aurora Historical Society includes a story from the San Francisco newspaper. Ray Demmitt's statistics come from baseball-reference.com. Marcia Mount, Michels's granddaughter, shared family memories, lent me many of the photos and consented to having me retell a story that she considers ghoulish. Send me an email (truetalesofaurora@gmail.com) and I'll reply with a postscript called "Whatever happened to the heads?"

Beacon-News. "Answer Lincoln Self Defense Pleas With Charge of Murder." January 14, 1924.

———. "Bank Deposits in Aurora Set New Record." April 6, 1923.

———. "Chief Michels on Force 40 Years Today." June 30, 1927.

———. "Chief Michels to Retire in the Spring." February 16, 1928.

———. "Crowds Turn Out as Mayor Drive Starts." April 4, 1923.

———. "Drink is Make in 1,000 Homes, Michels Thinks." April 8, 1923.

———. "Find Byron Shoup's Watch." January 15, 1924.

———. "Finds Heads of Mrs. Lincoln and Shoup in Stone Blocks." January 26, 1924.

———. "Get a Jury to Try Lincoln Case." January 23, 1925.

———. "How Lincoln Framed Alibis After Killing." January 14, 1924.

———. "Hunt Mrs. Lincoln and Her Brother." June 13, 1923.

———. "Lawyer's Body, Wife Still Missing." May 1, 1923.

———. "Lincoln Angry At Verdict, Declares He Will Appeal." February 11, 1925.

———. "Lincoln Confesses." January 14, 1923.

———. "Lincoln Cunning Coward, Abbott Says." January 24, 1925.

———. "Lincoln Feared Red Haired Man, His Son Says." May 1, 1923.

———. "Lincoln Found, Alive," June 12, 1923.

———. "Lincoln Goes Over Scene of Alleged Crimes." January 19, 1924.

———. "Lincoln 'Just A Liar' State Witnesses Say." February 7, 1925.

———. "Lincoln Murder Trial On Morrow." January 14, 1925.

———. "Lincoln Says His Wife Is Alive." January 21, 1924.

———. "Lincoln Stares As He's Condemned." February 8, 1925.

———. "Lincoln Tells Life History to Reporter." January 27, 1924.

———. "'Milo Durand' is Hunted in Lincoln Case." May 9, 1923.

———. "Move to Arrest Lincoln's Wife, Brother." May 3, 1923.

———. "Murder Farmer, Steal Body." April 30, 1923.

———. "New Confession By Lincoln, No Help To Police." January 23, 1924.

———. "Plane Writes Lucky Strike in Sky Tonight." April 28, 1923.

———. "Relationship of Warren and the Great Lincoln." January 15, 1924.

———. "Sheriff Says Lincoln Story May Be A Dream." June 14, 1923.

———. "Think Three Were At Lincoln Home." May 2, 1923.

———. "Two Mayoralty Candidates on Stump Tonight." April 5, 1923.

———. "Warren Lincoln Is Arrested." January 13, 1923.

Chicago Tribune. "Lincoln Admits Killing Wife." January 14, 1924.

———. "Lincoln Faces Death or Asylum." January 27, 1924.

———. "Lincoln Played Cards as Fire Burned Victims." January 29, 1924.

———. "Lincoln Washed and Covered Tracks." January 14, 1924.

———. "Seize 'Slain Man' as Slayer." January 13, 1924.

———. "Warren Lincoln Guilty; Gets Life in Prison." February 10, 1925.

Ray Demmitt Player Page. Last modified 2012. http://www.baseball-reference.com/players/d/demmira01.shtml

Smith, Stephen. *America's Greatest Brands* 1. New York: America's Greatest Brands, 1997.

Taylor, Merlin Moore. *True Detective Mysteries.* New York: Macfadden, July 1929.

William B. Tubbs. "A Lincoln In Name Only." *For the People* (Summer 2000).

The Two Burials of Three-Fingered Hamilton

Most of this story was built from the original FBI file on Volney Davis obtained by FOIA request; a Minnesota Eighth Circuit Court of Appeals decision online at Justia.com; and stories in August 1935 editions of the *Beacon-News.* Confirmation of some details about the recovery of Hamilton's body came from the *Chicago Tribune* archives. The Wisconsin Historical

Society website provided context for the Little Bohemia battle. Finally, the context for Dillinger and Hamilton's criminal lifestyle, and the anecdote about being turned down by Capone's gang, came from Bryan Burroughs's excellent book, *Public Enemies.*

Beacon-News. "Agents Still Hunt Davis in This Section." February 9, 1935.
———. "Escaped Kidnapper Lived in Aurora as 'Curley Hansen.'" February 8, 1935.
———. "Find Body in Shallow Grave." August 29, 1935.
———. "Hunted Pals of Dillinger Once Kane Prisoners." July 24, 1934.
———. "Jesse Doyle, of Bremer Case in Flight Here." February 7, 1935.
———. "Nab Gangster in Austin; Rush Him to St. Paul." June 3, 1935.
———. "Pauper Grave for Man Who Stole Fortune." August 30, 1935.
———. "Sister Buries Hamilton in Oswego Grave." August 31, 1935.
———. "Volney Davis Betrayed by Girl in Austin." June 4, 1935.
———. "Volney Davis is Hunted as Boy Kidnapper." June 2, 1935.
Burrough, Bryan. *Public Enemies: America's Greatest Crime Wave and the Birth of the FBI, 1933–1934.* London: Penguin Books, 2004.
Chicago Tribune. "Desperado Who Escaped Agents is Volney Davis." February 9, 1935.
———. "Gangster Davis Speedily Tells Bremer Guilt." June 4, 1935.
———. "Interment at Dawn." September 1, 1935.
———. "John Hamilton's Death in Chicago Told at Inquest." August 30, 1935.
———. "U.S. Agents Dig Up Hamilton's Body at Oswego." August 29, 1935.
———. "U.S. Grand Jury Indicts 22 For Plot on Bremer." January 25, 1935.
———. "Volney Davis, Karpis' Outlaw Pal, Captured." June 3, 1935.
———. "Volney Davis, Outlaw of '30s, Wins Hearing." January 26, 1954.
Dictionary of Wisconsin History. Last updated 2012. http://www.wisconsinhistory.org/dictionary/
"Volney Davis, Appellant, v. United States of America, Appellee." JustiaUSLaw.com. Last modified 2012. http://law.justia.com/cases/federal/appellate-courts/F2/226/834/297653/

SONNY BOY'S BLUES

Billy Boy Arnold, Michael Baker, Adam Gussow, Bill Donaghue and Billy Altman were all interviewed in 2012. Baker provided most of the historical notes on Sonny Boy's early life, including copies of his obituary and information on Sonny Boy's childhood. Information about Sonny Boy's murder came from the original Chicago Police Department police files, obtained by FOIA request. Copies of the set list for Sonny Boy's Aurora recordings were made available by the Aurora Historical Society. I relied on several books for context on the blues, including *Conversation with the Blues* by Paul Oliver, *The History of the Blues* by Francis Davis and *The NPR Curious Listener's Guide to Blues* by David Evans. *Harmony, Harps and Heavy Breathers* provided historical context for the instrument. The Alan Lomax interviews with Sonny Boy Williamson were retrieved from The Association for Cultural Equity website. Lomax's book, *The Land Where the Blues Began* provided context for the interviews.

Beacon-News. "Aurora Becomes the Home of the Blues this Weekend." June 14, 2001.
———. "Dedicate New Aurora Leland Hotel Wednesday Night." February 7, 1928.
———. "Prayed for Rain Now Against It." May 5, 1937.
Courier. "John Lee 'Sonny Boy' Williamson: Blues Innovator," February 1991.
Cultural Equity. Last modified 2012. www.culturalequity.org.
Davis, Francis. *The History of the Blues: The Roots, The Music, The People From Charley Patton to Robert Cray.* New York: Hyperion, 1995.
Evans, David. *The NPR Curious Listener's Guide to Blues*. New York: Perigree Trade, 2005.
Field, Kim. *Harmony Harps and Heavy Breathers: The Evolution of the People's Instrument*. New York: Cooper Square Press, 1993.
Lomax, Alan. *The Land Where the Blues Began*. New York: Pantheon Books, 1993.
Metro Forum. "I Knew 'Sonny Boy.'" December 20, 1989–January 2, 1990.
Paul Oliver. *Conversation With the Blues*. Cambridge, MA: Cambridge University Press, 1997.
Salles, Andre. "Legendary Downtown Blues Haven Turned into Lofts." *Beacon-News*, September 24, 2009.

LEAP YEAR LADIES

This story was constructed through *Beacon-News* stories (Leap Years 1940–84) and the personal memories of Audre' Grometer.

MEDAL OF HONOR

The personal details of Truemper's life came from *Beacon-News* stories and the memories of Ann Prestero. The main story of the mission and the crew's heroics came from 1944 issues of the *Beacon-News* and *Chicago Tribune*. As cited in the story, several details of what was happening inside the plane come from the incredible book *Valor at Polebrook: The Last Flight of Ten Horsepower* by Rick School and Jeff Rogers.

Beacon-News. "Correspondents Retell Story of Flyer's Heroic Death." March 12, 1944.

————. "General Will Read Mother Son's Citation." July 3, 1944.

————. "Mother Will Receive Medal Awarded Son." July 2, 1944.

————. "Mrs. Truemper Given Highest Honor For Son." July 5, 1944.

————. "Notify Parents Lt. Truemper Dies in Action." March 2, 1944.

Chicago Tribune. "Arnold Stresses Attrition by Air." February 21, 1944.

————. "Aurora Mother Given Top U.S. Medal for Son." July 5, 1944.

————. "Heroic Aurora Flyer Awarded Highest Medal." July 3, 1944.

————. "New Village Names Streets After 3 Heroes." August 29, 1948.

————. "Two Killed Trying to Save Fortress." February 22, 1944.

————. "2,000 U.S. Planes Smash German Aircraft Plants." February 21, 1944.

School, Rick and Jeff Rogers. *Valor at Polebrook: The Last Flight of Ten Horsepower.* Amherst, Wisconsin: Palmer Publications, 2000.

FROM BOXCARS TO BEARS

Most of the information in this story came from personal interviews with Pat Perez, Matt Perez, Michael Nila, Tony Torres, Lupe Vargas, Lou Beatus and Robert Brent. Other details on the Perez biography and the boxcar communities came from various stories in the *Beacon-News*. A story in the September 29, 1945 *Chicago Tribune* provided details of Perez's first training camp. The information on Perez's football career came from *Athletes Remembered: Mexicano/Latino Professional Football Players, 1929–1970* by Mario Longoria and football-reference.com. The PBS documentary "The Storm that Swept Mexico" was helpful for understanding the context of the Mexican Revolution. Finally, Aurora University professor Dr. Susan Palmer has done amazing work documenting life in the Aurora boxcar community. Her article provided invaluable details about Manuel Perez and the boxcar life.

Beacon-News. "Perez Aims for Another New Career." December 3, 1978.

DeFour, Matthew. "Perez Intersection Dedication a First for Latino Community." *Beacon-News*, October 13, 2005.

Donahue, Ann. "An Officer of Strength, Compassion." *Beacon-News*, February 10, 1999.

———. "Family, Friends, Peers Pay Last Respects to Pete Perez." *Beacon-News*, February 11, 1999.

Falcon, Penny, "Tracking the Latino Movement into the Fox Valley." *Beacon-News*, March 20, 1994.

Haase, Roald, "Kramer Taps Perez for Undersheriff." *Beacon-News*, July 25, 1978.

Hanley, Matt, "Pioneering Nila Family Honored." *Beacon-News*, July 9, 2009.

Longoria, Mario. *Athletes Remembered: Mexicano/Latino Professional Football Players, 1929–1970.* Austin, TX: Bilingual Press, 1997.

Mueller, Martha. "Deep Roots." *Beacon-News*, May 5, 1991.

Palmer, Susan L. "The Community-Building Experiences of Mexicans in Aurora, Illinois, 1915–1935." 2005, http://dig.lib.niu.edu/ISHS/ishs-2005autumn/ishs-2005autumn125.pdf

PBS. "The Storm that Swept Mexico." 2011.

Prell, Edward. "Bears Work Like Beavers in Last Drill at Camp." *Chicago Tribune*, September 29, 1945.

Wang, Justina. "Aurora Families to be Honored for Their Struggles, Courage." *Beacon-News*, September 16, 2005.

KENNEDY AND NIXON

This story was constructed entirely from the archives of the *Beacon-News* (July–October 1960). And, as cited, Wilma Howard, Tom Weisner, Jean Jackson and Kathleen Kort also provided personal details.

About the Author

M att Hanley grew up in Hoffman Estates, Illinois. He earned his bachelor's and master's degrees in journalism from the University of Illinois at Urbana–Champaign. He worked at the *Elburn Herald* and *LaSalle News Tribune* before being hired by the *Aurora Beacon-News* in 2003. For the last seven years, he has covered crime, runaway chickens and obscure historical stories for the *Beacon-News*. This is his first book, and hopefully not his last. To contact him, email truetalesofaurora@gmail.com.

Visit us at
www.historypress.net